This book in its entirety is dedicated to my loving parents and brother & wife. Their unconditional love, support, guidance and infinite wisdom is the foundation to my **Inspired Success.**

INSPIRED SUCCESS

DESIGNING YOUR OWN DEFINITION OF SUCCESS

RASHAN SENANAYAKE

Contributors

Tim Sifontes-Holzberger from Linkedwood Publishing for the amazing guidance, content creation as well as editing and proofing (2nd Edition).

Anna Ball from Dot & Quill Communications for her amazing contributions in the development of this book as well as editing and proofing (1st Edition).

Melanie Kilby from Kismet Art Design for the beautiful diagrams and Illustrations you will enjoy.

Inspired Design Australia Pty Ltd. for the awesome cover design.

Maverick Chang from Flare Media for the amazing cover photo.

Daniel Jeffs from MyIdealHealth for the creative writing and insightful health tips.

The legend that is Ian Healy, for a magnificent foreword.

All the wonderful and inspiring individuals who have reviewed the book.

Disclaimer

This publication offers information, insights, guidance, techniques and/or programs of a general nature which should not be treated as professional, medical, allied health or psychological advice.

The reader:

1. should seek appropriate advice from a qualified professional or practitioner before adopting or implementing any of the suggestions, techniques and/or programs;
2. is solely responsible for determining the suitability of the information, insights, guidance, techniques and/or programs for their use and any use of the information, insights, guidance, techniques and/or programs is at the reader's own risk; and
3. acknowledges that use of the information, insights, guidance, techniques and/or programs does not guarantee a particular outcome or result.

Acknowledgements

This book humbly acknowledges the use of publications or parts thereof outside of the author's own content. Where another author or speaker has been quoted, it has been referenced.

These other publications include direct quotes, paraphrased excerpts of published works and anecdotes that belong to others and their stories, and in no way are these claimed to be the original works of this book's authors or publishers.

The author would like to personally thank each individual who has been referenced within this book, making this "gateway book" possible with a holistic collection of wisdom, moments, lessons, advice, and mantras. It is the author's intention that the readers of this book will seek out the referenced books, authors, and role models as learning opportunities.

CONTENTS

Inspired success
verb

The act of designing one's life and actions to meet your own definition of success.

ORIGIN
Late 20th Century, Colombo, Sri Lanka.

"

Everyone has to start off with developing
his or her own definition of success.

And when we have these specific expectations of
ourselves, we are more likely to live up to them.

Ultimately, it's not what you get or even
what you give... it's what you become.

Mary Gates
*Bill Gate's Mother, American Businesswoman, Executive,
Civic Activist and School Teacher*

FOREWORD BY IAN HEALY

Former Australian International Cricket Player, Sports Australia Hall of Fame, Entrepreneur, Father

Designing YOUR blueprint for success is how I interpret Rashan's manuscript. What an amazing selection of crucial characteristics for an individual to master! Even the closest of friends, or even twins, will have different images of what success looks like for them. Rashan starts out discovering what one might define as success.

Is it a high level of performance in something? Is it happiness? Is it being confident enough to be inquisitive in life, or to be in a position to be thankful and considerate?

I've lived with some cricketing legends (and I mean the very best) who –
- Did not even set goals.
- Couldn't sit still long enough to even complete our team planning sessions.
- Yet, some prepared copious strategic notes for themselves and others, which is what enabled them all to perform consistently well.

Discovering and doing what works for you is the important part of performance. There is no right or wrong here, it's all yours to design.

Awareness of human characteristics is great and Rashan thoroughly details these attributes through these pages -- but executing the characteristics you desire is harder to achieve. Which parts of this book are relevant to me, is the key question?

Knowing what parts of each characteristic you are lacking in, competent in, or great at, is a fantastic step, but using that understanding to then improve yourself requires discipline and motivation.

Rashan Senanayake investigates so many great qualities in this success bible. Are you **fulfilled**? It's easier to know why we're not finding joy than why we are. The skill here is to be aware in your good times of what you're feeling, so that you can maintain this level of engagement and happiness.

I've always rated **time management** as the most important trait to possess. A clear, well prepared mind is my key to success. I am then in control, not my thoughts.

In my cricket playing days, I worked out that I even needed to plan for excessive emotion on tense days, rather than have it disturb what was important to performing well under pressure, namely the repetition of basic skills.

Planning to be really busy at times is good, or planning breaks also provides control. It's this control that enables me to deal with **stress** (both good and bad) at least adequately. Stress is another quality in life, well considered in this book.

One trait that Australians now need to be taught or reminded of is **resilience**, which annoys me a little. Our indigenous heritage, the Colonial arrivals and battles fought right through the World Wars and modern wars; Australians are renowned for being resilient. It should never be diluted and taken for granted, but I fear it is no longer embedded within our DNA.

Another modern skill for consistently high performance is to '**be present**', undistracted, enthusiastic, and constructive. Giving value to others rather than just absorbing their wisdom and fun. Separate time for the distractions of email, phone, and messages, so you don't bog down, churning on the spot as opposed to moving forwards personally.

My time in sporting teams meant I spent much time analysing the combinations of personalities we had selected and how best to combine players for high performance.

Goal driven players, emotional flair players, thinkers and list makers craving information, or sheer naturals must ALL avoid overthinking. It is destructive to clear headed performance.

The power of positive doing is better than the power of positive thinking. Be aware quickly when you're overthinking and snap out of it by doing heaps more than you're doing at present. Get going with actions.

Rashan has done an outstanding job in pulling together so many life learnings and strategies. It is a book which some will read from end to end, others will pick at topic by topic rather than attempting to digest it all at once. It just might cover topics familiar to you, but do not fret. There are learnings aplenty and it may also be incredibly useful for someone you know, or provide you information to help a friend to cope better with future challenges that might arise.

Self-awareness never stops. Our moods and attitudes change with age and the life changes we experience. Working out why we are thinking and feeling the things we are takes continuous thought and effort.

The resources of this success blueprint are incredible. Human traits and strategies to enable happiness, success, fulfilment, and control, are explained perfectly. Teaching and learning this stuff is still easier than doing it.

Knowledge can be power to take action.

I hope you can enjoy your improved wellbeing.

Ian H

WHAT IS INSPIRED SUCCESS?

Despite the clever little definition at the start of this book, you're still probably wondering, what is 'Inspired Success'?

Inspired Success is the guide to the creative act of intentionally designing your life, to enable your own goals, milestones, vision and missions – all on your own terms.

This is for you, by you! It can get incredibly personal and requires you to reflect, and investigate yourself, your habits and goals, and open your heart and mind.

(Easier said than done!)

Before we get into the nitty gritty, let's cut to the chase! Success is not about how much money is in your bank account or even your net worth. There are many financially successful people out there that may lead a successful life on the surface, but have very little substance and meaning. Where you are wealthy in one area, you may be poor in others. One's Instagram account is not a measure of success.

"Success is the progressive realisation of a worthy ideal"

Success to me (and you may or may not agree with me - but since you have picked up this book, read on with an open heart) is… happiness.

A successful life contains wealth not just financially, but also wealth in time, wealth in health, wealth in contentment, wealth in happiness, wealth in relationships, wealth in options and choice.

Many aspire to be successful financially, have a lot of money – become a big shot! Drive an expensive car, go on expensive holidays and wear designer brands… why?

(Absolutely nothing wrong with that, by the way)

However, imagine for a second that you are a CEO earning a million dollars a year and can buy a designer home with all the latest gadgets, with an Instagram account that has a few million followers from the lifestyle you've shown to the world – but if you have no time to enjoy it, enjoy your family and friends, you're constantly stressed working 24/7, always on your phone – are

you successful?
Perhaps…

Perhaps not…

It is about finding YOUR **definition** of success, to be wealthy all around.

This book will give you a guide that has been designed and developed during the author's own personal journey, experience and learnings to date. This book will be sharing valuable life experiences, learnings, knowledge, insights and even the mistakes along the way with actionable practices learned from the best of the best this world has to offer.

This book is about designing a step-by-step, brick-by-brick approach to life design. Just imagine for a second that you were to build a beautiful house from scratch, with your own hands. A house for you to call home, to live in. You wouldn't simply start to lay bricks and build walls. That would result in the structure being unsafe to live in and the end outcome may not reflect what you wanted in the first place. However, this is what most people do with their life, their entire life. You would begin with a plan in place, design, define, document and then enter the building process. Within the building process, you would start with laying a solid foundation first, then the structure, then the walls, roof, doors, windows and so on. Building your walls, you would lay one brick at a time. In doing so, lay that one brick as carefully and beautifully as you possibly can.

This is the same for your life – you would design, define, and document, and then enter the building process. Within the building process, you would start off laying a solid foundation *(your self-awareness)*, then the structure *(your body)*, then the walls, roof, doors, windows *(everything else)*. Building each of these elements, you would lay one brick *(or one small task within an overall plan)* at a time. You would lay this brick as perfectly, intentionally and mindfully as possible. Consistently doing so, day-in-day-out, you will one day have a beautiful structure that you can call your life – a successful one, designed and constructed by you, for you, on your own terms.

So, let's read on...

Success. What exactly is it?

Today, we live in a golden age of technology, information, and a fast-paced digital world. This is an era humanity has looked forward to, dreamed of and worked towards for thousands of years. But since it's arrived, we pretty much take it for granted. If you are living in the first world – countries such as the USA, Australia, Canada, UK – you are most likely fortunate enough to live as a part of the richest population that has ever existed on the face of the earth. These are the lands of endless opportunity for everyone. But what is the reality?

Let's take 100 random people who start with even odds and resources at the age of 25. Do you have any idea what will happen to these people by the time they are at the age of 65? These 100 people believe they are going to be successful. If you ask any of them *"Do you want to be a success?"* they would tell you that they do and you would notice the eagerness towards life – with a certain sparkle in their eye and courage to soldier on. At this point – life seems like a motivating journey. No one expects or aims to be broke or restricted in life.

But by the time they are 65 – only one will be 'rich'. Four will be financially independent. Five will still be working – pay cheque to pay cheque. Fifty-four will be broke and dependent on the government pension or a relative. Now think for a moment, out of the 100 people how do only five achieve their financial goals? Why is the failure rate so high? What happened to the ambition that existed when they were 25? What happened to the dreams, the hopes, the plans? Why is there such a large discrepancy between what they intended to do and what was actually accomplished?

Well, to understand this, we must first define success. Success that, on average, only 5% of people will achieve. So here it is:

Success
noun
"Success is the progressive realisation of a worthy ideal"

If a person is working towards a predetermined goal and knows where they are going – that person is a success. If they are not doing that – they are a failure.

"Success is the progressive realisation of a worthy ideal"

Rollo May, a distinctive psychiatrist wrote a life changing book called *"Man's Search for Himself"* in 1953. In this book he says:

❝❝

"The opposite of courage in our society is not cowardice, it is conformity"

Rollo May
(The Man's Search for Himself, 1953)

Although this was quoted from a book published in 1953, this is exactly the trouble of humanity. The road block. The glass ceiling, which even today presents as conformity. People acting like everyone else, following the crowd, without a vision, consuming without understanding and ultimately 'living' without knowing why, or even where they are going.

Let's take a closer look – out of the 7.8 billion people on the face of this world, about 790 million people are 65 years of age or over. From which about 750 million out of the 790 million people are broke, or are financially dependent on someone else for life's necessities. What happened?!

Most of us, as children, learn to read by the time we are 7. If we are lucky and live in a first world country this may be lowered to 5 years old. We enter higher education by the age of 17-20. Most of us will enter the workforce and begin to earn a living by the time we are 25. Usually by that time, we are not only making a living, but we are also starting to support a family. Yet by the time we are 65 we have not learned how to be financially independent in the most golden age of humanity! Why?

Because we conform. We are sheep – sheep that follow the pack. Even if it's taking us in totally the wrong direction!

On the contrary, if we started conforming to the 5% that do succeed, this would result in a fast progressing civilization. The trouble is that we are acting like the wrong percentage group – the 95% that don't succeed. Now why do these people conform? Well, they don't really know! Even if you ask them…

There is, however, a distinct pattern to their behaviour and mindset. Most of the people who conform believe their lives are shaped by circumstances. By things that happened 'to them'. By external factors. Therefore, they see no choice but to conform and follow.

There have been many studies and surveys that consistently prove the same pattern since the 1950's – when the respondents were asked *"Why do you work?"* or *"Why do you get up in the morning?"*, 19 out of 20 had no idea (on average of course!). Answers mainly showed the same pattern that points to: *"Everyone goes to work in the morning"* and therefore is the reason they do it – because everyone else is doing it.

Ask yourself:

"Why do you work?"

_____

_____

_____

_____

_____

"Why do you get up in the morning?"

_____

_____

_____

_____

_____

Now, let's get back to our definition of success and take a look at exactly **who** is successful. The only person that succeeds is the person who is progressively realising a worthy ideal. They are the people who say, *"I am going to become this, by this date!"* and then begin to work towards that goal. They may not know exactly how to get there, but they will work to find that out for sure!

Let me tell you who the successful people in this world are – a success is the school teacher who teaches at school because that's what they wanted to do. A success is a woman who is a wife and mother, because she wanted to be a wife and mother and owns her choices and decisions. A success is the man who runs their own cafe because that's what they always wanted to do. A success is the salesman who wants to be top-notch and grow and build both the company brand and his own. A success is anyone doing a deliberately predetermined job because that's what they decided to do – consciously and deliberately. But only 5% of the working population does this!

I have personally searched for answers to find out exactly why this happens. What are the variables, the causes and effects, the context, the mindset, the circumstances, the values, the attributes and the details? Is there a formula which, if followed, can guarantee a person becoming a success – if they know about it and how to use it?

Well I believe there is! This book aims to outline exactly that.

Have you noticed a man who becomes successful will continue to become successful? On the other hand, have you noticed how a man who fails will continue to fail? Ever heard someone describe another by saying *"everything they touch seems to turn to gold"*, or *"they have the magic touch"*? Well, let me tell you that there is no 'magic touch'. It is because of goals (not gold) – some of us have them, some don't. People with goals succeed, because they know where they are going and take actionable steps to achieve that goal.

Now think of a ship about to set sail to a wonderful island paradise – they have the entire journey mapped out and planned with a GPS tracking system in place (even with a fail-safe backup system!) The Captain and the crew know exactly where they're sailing and how long it will take and what to do. They have a definite goal. They even have contingencies, life rafts, consistently working on their ship's structural maintenance – just in case they face any challenges, obstacles, or even if they hit an iceberg – learning from the Titanic of course. What are the chances of them reaching their destination and enjoying a wonderful journey on their way to an island paradise?

9,999/10,000 that they will arrive safely at their destination and hit their goal.

Now let's take another ship. Just like the first, but let's not put a crew on it or even a Captain to lead the journey. Let's give it no aiming point. No goal. No destination. We just start the engines and just let it go. I think you will agree with me that if it even gets out of the harbour, that will be considered a lucky day or perhaps it will sink or wind up on some deserted beach as a wreck. It can't go anywhere, because it has no destination, guidance or even a fail safe.

This is the same with a human being. With you and me. I know which boat I'd rather sail on.

It was once said that:

66

*"The human race is fixed – not to prevent the strong from winning,
but to prevent the weak from losing".*

Anonymous

This is why it is easy to make a living today. It takes no particular brains or talent to make a living and support a family, receive higher education or become comfortable. So, we have a plateau of so-called 'security' if that's what a person is looking for – but we do have to decide how high above this plateau we want to aim for. Most expect a higher outcome by conforming to the masses.

If you start to understand what I have laid out for you in this book, from this moment onwards your life will never be the same again.

You will suddenly find that good luck just seems to be attracted to you. You will seem to have more energy. The things you want will just seem to fall in line. You will be happier... doubt, fear... well they will be things of the past! This is Inspired Success.

"

Every bit of knowledge unravelled in this book had to be found, refined and designed to fit. With so much information out there now, it's getting harder and harder to find the right information that applies directly to young adults and young professionals.

This is exactly what this book offers
- Just the right information we need,
but straight to the point!

Rashan Senanayake
@rashansenanayake
www.RashanSenanayake.com

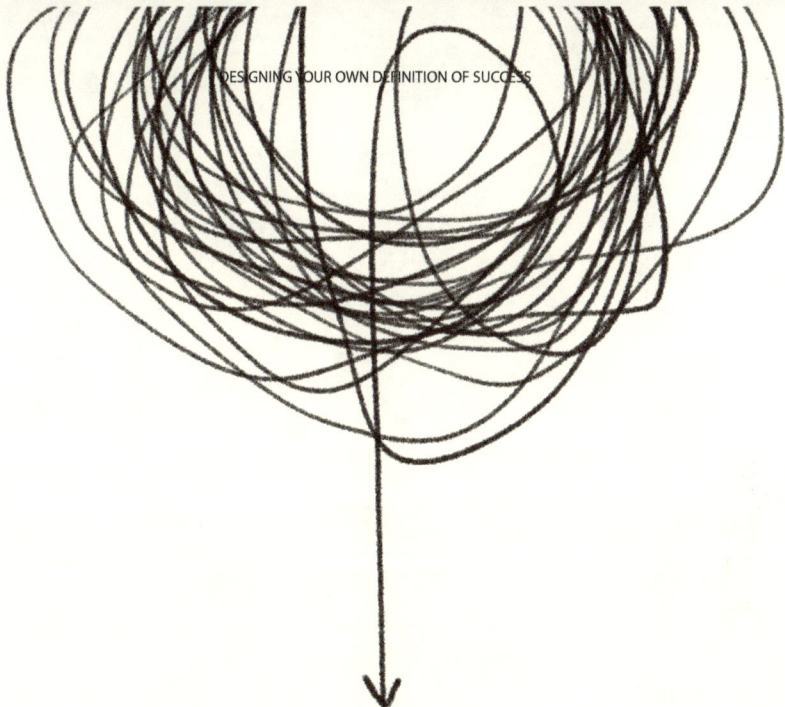

PART 1

WHY?

1

PART 1: **WHY?**

This is where we start. This is the root of understanding the cause and effect.

CHAPTER 1: **WHY?**

If you have been one of my students in the past, you would have definitely heard me ask "why?" a thousand times. Whether it's with regard to a design justification, life decision, or simply why you want to have chocolate ice cream over vanilla.

(Chocolate, hands down by the way!)

Starting with the why (*also one of my favourite books by Simon Sinek*) is the base foundation for anything in life. Our morals, values, mindset, and in turn our motivation and action stems from the why.

But here's the key thing – it's not just about asking "why?" one time and then moving on. Your why is something you need to revisit, time and again, especially when life takes unexpected turns. Think about it as a checkpoint, something you can always return to when you feel lost, overwhelmed, or just unsure about your next move. Whether you're deciding on a new job or simply figuring out how to spend your weekend, grounding yourself in your personal why can help you navigate those tricky waters.

Why am I studying at university?
Why should I spend time with them?
Why am I looking for work?

Why should I go to that event?
Why should I work out?
Why am I on this career path?
Why am I using this social media platform?
Why...?

The beauty of asking *"why"* consistently is that it creates clarity, not just in big life decisions like career moves, but even in the smallest parts of our day-to-day lives. When you constantly ask why, you're not just accepting things as they are – you're giving yourself the space to get inspired, to question the status quo, and to make choices that align with your real values. This is where you really start building a life that's not only successful, but actually meaningful to you.

Our mindset is constantly reformed based on how strong and clear our why is, with regards to any aspect of life. This also means that the stronger your why, the stronger your motivation is and the stronger your actions towards a particular goal. Lack of motivation is usually linked to an undefined why, or even a lack of why.

Now, let's talk about the **"Golden Circle".** Simon Sinek *(that author I mentioned a minute ago)* introduced this way of thinking in a TED Talk back in 2010. His model encourages us to start with the why before moving on to the how and what *(yep, I learnt a lot from this guy!).* It's like building a house – you don't start by putting on the roof or choosing the carpets. You pour the foundation first. In the case of your own Golden Circle, your why is that foundation. And just like a house won't stand without a strong base, your goals – as well as your how and what, in Sinek's terms – won't hold up if you don't have a clear understanding of why you're pursuing them.

In turn, the stronger your actions are, the higher value you place on the why, and therefore it becomes a higher priority in your life. *(Now comes the best part!)* If it is a high priority in your life, then all of a sudden TIME will become more available and nothing can stop you from achieving that goal or task or milestone in your life.

(Easier said than done! But it can be done – it's simply an intentional design process.)

The Golden Circle and finding your why also mesh beautifully with the Japanese concept of Ikigai *(which is a little teaser for later in the book...).* While the Golden Circle encourages you to start with why to drive motivation, Ikigai adds layers of personal meaning. When you combine these two frameworks, you create a highly personal, resilient roadmap to success that isn't just about hitting goals, but about finding fulfilment along the way.

Ikigai brings in that holistic touch that, for me, makes this whole 'why' thing click into place. It's about discovering your purpose at a deeper level, beyond ambition or external validation. While the Golden Circle helps you articulate your why, Ikigai asks you to consider how that why fits into a life that's authentically yours. Together, along with the other tools we cover in this book, they serve as a toolkit to guide both career and life choices, making sure that what you're pursuing isn't just achievable but truly worthwhile to your life's 'design'.

When it comes to your personal why, it's important to view it as a checkpoint at both a macro and micro scale. At the macro level, it can help guide major life decisions, like choosing a career path, a family lifestyle, or even where to live. But your why is just as important on a micro level, affecting the smaller choices you make daily, like how you spend your time, what you eat, or what kind of furniture you buy. Each of these decisions reflects a part of your values, so regularly revisiting your why on both levels can help you live more intentionally.

Having a clear why doesn't just help you get through life with purpose – it can also make you a more inspiring and effective leader. Leaders who know and can communicate their why are better able to connect with others on a deeper level, building trust and loyalty with your team. When you can properly frame your why, you're not only guiding your own choices but also giving others a reason to follow your vision *(and don't worry, we'll definitely be exploring this more later!)*.

So let's say you're in a job or class that isn't quite lighting your fire, and you're wondering whether to stick with it or start something new. What's your why? Maybe you're there because it pays the bills *(or will in the future)*, and you need to support yourself or your family. That's a valid why, but it might not be enough to sustain you in the long run. Now ask yourself again: what's the deeper reason? Is it because this role is a stepping stone to a bigger dream? Or maybe it's giving you skills you'll need to succeed the way you want to one day? The more you refine your why *(which we'll talk about in the next chapter…)*, the more motivated you'll be to either find ways to make your current situation work or take the leap into something new.

If we put all this into context of the simple scenario of *Jeremy*, a final year MBA student approaching an assignment deadline...

Jeremy: Why should I finish this project today? Because it's due tomorrow.

- **Why:** To pass the assignment and pass the course and graduate to land my dream job and kick ass at life!
- **Motivation:** I have to finish it today, so I can complete the assignment.

- **Action:** Finish the assignment today!
- **Value:** Very High!
- **Priority:** Very High!
- **Time:** Nothing else matters!
- **Result:** Completion of task, above all else.

This is an easy scenario. Easy to relate to because most of us have gone through it, whether at school, at university, or at work. Usually with someone telling you exactly what, and why to do something. If we take a closer look, why do students and young professionals always get things done when there is time pressure? Because it takes the *'choice of action'* out of the equation – there is no longer time to watch that TV show or go out with friends or go hang gliding *(as you would!)*, or even procrastinate. So, things get done!

This is human nature.

But I have always seen a small percentage of students and young professionals who complete their work/project beyond the norm, maintain a social life, play sports, go to the gym, spend time with family, and still sleep for 7+ hours every night!

(What?! How is this possible? You may ask.)

Is this because they are smarter than the average person? Is it because they are having an extra hour in the day that we don't know about? Certainly, it may seem that way…

The answer to both of those questions is – NO! They are not smarter, and they have the same 24 hours that everyone on this planet has.

The only difference is that they have a stronger and clearer why. This helps them identify priorities, which in turn allows them to action things with equal priority – same as Jeremy in the last 24 hours of the assignment deadline. When you have a strong why, or most importantly can formulate a stronger why, it is the solid foundation to designing your definition of a successful life.

If we put this into the context of Jeremy (the same MBA student from earlier), but this time he is also working a part-time bartending job while studying full time!

Jeremy: Why do I need this bartending job? Because…

- **Why:** I need to fund my basic needs like food, rent, and lifestyle, as well as my tuition funds.
- **Motivation:** I will work hard to keep this job and get a promotion to

manage the bar. That way I can earn more, work less hours, and gain more flexibility for my MBA.

- **Action:** Go to work every day and outperform everyone!
- **Value:** Very desirable and Very High!
- **Priority:** Very High!
- **Time:** Nothing else matters!
- **Result:** High quality work ethic, passing grades and a lifestyle he desires.

It seems so simple... well, easier said than done! However, personally speaking, I have applied this technique to every single aspect of my own life. Whether in my own business ventures, sports, teaching, career, family life, love life... anything. Why? The principle is the same and can be applied to every context.

The important thing to understand and believe is that this is a learned behaviour. It is not an inherent talent or hereditary – it is learned, trained and practised. Jeremy has learnt to design his own life by refining his behaviours, actions and thoughts, intentionally.

2

CHAPTER 2: **FIVE WHYS?**

Let's get down to the techniques. The next step of formulating and understanding a stronger why is understanding that your why can come in all shapes and sizes. For example, a simple why could be single-staged:

Why do I have to work out now? To lead a healthy lifestyle (or to get that beach bod? Or impress that special someone?).

This by itself is sometimes not strong enough to drive high motivation and massive action. When things get difficult, if your why is not strong enough, you may lose track of your motivation to move forward. For example, think of the above scenario, but after a long twelve-hour work day plus one hour commute with another early morning ahead of you.

Would you still work out? No! Not if you have a weak (or unresolved) why! It simply becomes a secondary priority and Netflix takes its place.

Yes! If you have a strong why! i.e. you want to achieve your goal, regardless of your circumstances or conflicting priorities.

(Remember! Tiredness is forgotten very quickly!)

So, to formulate a strong why, simply ask - why? Then why? Then why again? Then why once again? Until you get to the defined, central why at the core of yourself.

(Hope I didn't lose you there! Read the above sentence a few times, until it begins to make sense).

Think about a young kid, who's just developed enough to be asking questions and understanding the answers. They ask why, you tell them. They ask why that's the answer, so you tell them again. They ask again, and you're probably getting a bit frustrated, or saying *"I don't know"* – which will probably be met with another why. The difference between that kid and you right now? Not much! That kid is trying to understand the world around them – you're trying to understand yourself, your motivations, your needs and wants.

These whys, the ones that drill down to the core of who you are, are easy for us to gloss over for most of our lives. They're definitely in there, inside us, but really looking at them can be pretty confronting! But it doesn't always have to be. This is why we start by asking about the smaller things, and naturally, as you step through all five whys, it opens up to the greater truth that's really motivating your decisions.

Like this:

Why do I have to work out now? To be healthy or get fitter.
Why do I want to be healthy and fitter? To feel better.
Why do I need to feel better? To get more done and have more energy.
Why do I need to get more done and have more energy? To be able to work hard at my job, spend time with my loved ones and play soccer.
Why do I want to do all those things? To live my life to the fullest.

All of a sudden, doing those push-ups or making that phone call or coding that app seems like such an easy thing to do!

The beauty of the Five Whys technique is that it isn't just a process of asking questions – it's a tool for self-reflection. By breaking down a decision layer by layer, you can see the connection between your choices and your underlying values and get closer to the core of what truly matters. Over time, this regular reflection builds up a sort of *"cause and effect"* lens, which you can look through when you need to see whether a path or choice aligns with your own guiding principles. This reflection is the key to understanding if a choice is genuinely right for you.

Every time you move up a why-stage, it becomes stronger, and stronger, and stronger. Until you are at a point where all other excuses are heavily outweighed by your why. This is the key to finding unlimited amounts of motivation alongside sustainable change.

When used consistently, the Five Whys technique becomes an invaluable practice, like a personalised compass for making decisions. Regularly working through your five stages allows you to tap into the clarity and focus you need to design a life that fits your own definition of success. By making this technique part of your toolkit, you're equipping yourself with everything you need to stay connected to what truly matters.

When asking your Five Whys becomes second nature, the answer to your stage-one why questions can change:

Why do I have to work out now? To live my life to the fullest.

This answer is formulated, with a clear vision of all stages. This is through the practice of internally searching for answers, meditating, and reflecting within yourself. Until you get to a point where your vision is sharpened to view your why-stages clearly, take the time to go through the motion of consciously staging each why. It is like riding a bicycle – once you know how to do it, you will never forget it. This is called muscle memory. Similarly, your mind has muscle memory for various practices and thought processes.

Finally, it may not be five stages – it could be two stages, it could be fifteen stages. Each scenario is different to each individual. It is simply a matter of asking why until you get to the centre, and five is a good place to start.

Mindful practice tip: When you first begin asking your whys, you can easily get stuck in a loop, answering your own questions with the same answer. When you recognise yourself doing this, take a break and mindfully attempt to view it from another perspective and try again. No one in this world would start sprinting straight away at birth – you first crawl, then stand up, then walk a few steps, but fall many times, then walk, then jog, then sprint and finally refine your sprint to become the fastest you can be!

Just like that, procrastination is now a thing of the past...

TIME TO TAKE ACTION!

Check out the downloadable resources for this section
at www.rashansenanayake.com

"

Everyone's like 'overnight sensation'. It's not overnight. It's years of hard work.

Margot Robbie
Prolific International Actress & Film Producer

3

CHAPTER 3: **SMART GOALS**

Goals are part of every aspect of our lives. They are based around the decisions we make, our relationships, career milestones, and even your spare time – sometimes consciously, sometimes subconsciously. Without setting goals or objectives, everyday life can be described as a series of chaotic moments without any control or direction – it is a meaningless and purposeless life. Drifting… with no destination in mind. On the contrary, amazing accomplishments (like sending the first man to the moon) or the invention of a specific product (*like the introduction of the iPad)* are a result of a specific goal setting, mapped and achieved through a strong vision and why.

Nonetheless, I don't want to spend a lot of time on goals, because each of us has very different goals and desires. But whatever your goals might be, write them down and work to achieve them!

(Why? To write something down, you have to formulate a clear thought process. This is then followed up clearly defining your goals. This in turn will help you visualise it.)

I want to become an architect one day!
I want to be the highest run scorer next season!
I want to speak in front of 500 people next year!
I want to run a mile in under 1 minute!

I want to compose my own music and release an album!
I want to code my app and sell it on iTunes!
I want to write a book!
I want to start my own podcast!

Anything...

This is where SMART goals come into play.

SMART goal setting is a fairly common concept and strategy towards achieving specific goals in your life – it is an invaluable tool. It is a vehicle (*like a sports car!*) used for goal setting to fast-track various elements in your life.

In SMART goal setting, you're encouraged to break down goals into smaller, structured parts that you can take specific action on—keeping you on track and accountable along the way. But before diving into the mechanics, it's essential to identify the areas in your life you want to improve or progress. This can include personal aspects like health, relationships, finances, or hobbies, or professional elements like career progression, skill development, networking, and work-life balance. Clarity around these focus areas will make your goals more aligned and realistic, creating a smoother path to success.

SMART goal setting imparts structure, accountability, and trackability into your goals. Instead of a general goal (*I will be a director of my own company, someday!*), SMART goals allow you to create a specific, verifiable road map towards a certain goal or objective. It needs to outline specific milestones, with attainable, time-specific, and measurable targets.

SMART goals can be described as:

S-Specific
M-Measurable
A-Attainable
R-Relevant
T-Time-Specific

Let's break down these steps to make your SMART goals even more actionable:

1. Define Specific Goals
Be clear about what you want to achieve. For example:
- Personal: "*I want to lose 10 pounds*" instead of "*I want to get healthier.*"
- Professional: "*I want to complete a certification in data analysis*" instead of "*I want to improve my skills.*"

2. Make Goals Measurable
Identify how you will track progress.
- Personal: *"I will track my weight weekly and aim to lose 1 pound per week."*
- Professional: *"I will complete one module of my certification course every month."*

3. Ensure Goals Are Achievable
Make sure the goal is realistic based on your resources and constraints.
- Personal: *"I will exercise for 30 minutes, 3 times a week"* rather than *"I will run a marathon next month."*
- Professional: *"I will attend one industry networking event per month"* instead of *"I will meet 50 new professionals this month."*

4. Set Relevant Goals
Align the goal with your broader personal values or career objectives.
- Personal: *"Improving my fitness will help reduce stress and increase my energy for other areas of life."*
- Professional: *"This certification will improve my skills and help me qualify for a promotion."*

5. Set Time-Bound Goals
Establish a clear deadline or timeframe.
- Personal: *"I want to lose 10 pounds in the next 10 weeks."*
- Professional: *"I will complete my data analysis certification in six months."*

6. Break Goals into Smaller Tasks
For large goals, break them into manageable milestones.
- Personal: Break weight loss into daily or weekly exercise and diet adjustments.
- Professional: Break certification into weekly study hours or specific modules.

7. Review and Adjust Regularly
Periodically review progress and adjust your strategy if needed.
- Personal: *"If I'm not losing weight as expected, I'll consult a nutritionist."*
- Professional: *"If I fall behind in my certification, I'll adjust my study schedule."*

8. Celebrate Small Wins
Acknowledge and reward yourself for reaching milestones to stay motivated. An example of a SMART goal could look like this:
- Personal: *"I will lose 5 kgs by exercising 30 minutes 3 times a week and reducing calorie intake by 200 calories per day. I aim to achieve this in 10 weeks, tracking progress weekly."*
- Professional: *"I will earn a certification in data analysis by completing one module per month, finishing the entire course in six months, and dedicating*

5-hours weekly to studying."

By following these steps, you can ensure that your goals are clear, realistic, and aligned with your long-term vision for personal and professional success.

SMART goals make your dreams actionable, realistic, and trackable, and transform your vague hopes into clear plans. And with regular review and celebration of milestones, you're also building the confidence to keep moving forward in life! Just remember, achieving these goals is less about perfection and more about consistency.

So go on, get your **SMART** goals down on paper, and start the journey!

4

CHAPTER 4: **WHY & SMART GOALS**

So, how does your why and SMART goals relate? Well, when you have understood, formulated and clearly defined your why, this will derive various goals and achievement desires.

The SMART goals are the roadmap for your goal's achievement strategy. It's about bringing it to a realisation.

When your why and SMART goals are defined, set and combined, it is very difficult to lose focus and prevent yourself from achieving your goals *(however long or hard the process may be!)*. It safeguards the entire process. Even if you do stray away from your plan *(temporarily)*, or experience setbacks, it is very easy to get back on track and move forwards towards your goals, because you know what those goals are!

There are many other factors that come into play *(we will discuss these later in this book – such as time management and physical health to derive more energy)*, but to form a solid foundation in designing your definition of a successful life for yourself, is to start with the why and set SMART goals.

So when bridging your why and SMART goals, you're starting to create a clear, focused path that's unique to you. This brings us back to Ikigai. Your why lays the foundation for understanding purpose, but it's Ikigai that can add dimension, helping you refine and deepen your goals by ensuring they align with all aspects of your life. When you know both your why and your Ikigai, you're setting goals that not only make sense strategically but resonate personally, bringing you closer to a life that feels balanced and meaningful.

Let's consider a professional example: imagine your why is to create impactful, meaningful change in the education sector. With that why in mind, you might set a SMART goal of completing a specific certification or launching a piece of educational tech. However, by linking this goal to your Ikigai, you might realise that you also want this work to tap into your creative strengths (what you're good at), address an educational gap (what the world needs), and support a sustainable income (what you can be paid for). In doing so, you're not just aiming for professional success—you're building a career that aligns holistically with your values and skills.

We'll be exploring Ikigai in more depth in a later chapter, but for now, just know that all the tools we're covering here are designed to help you reach that harmonious state where your career, personal life, and goals are all aligned.

To make this whole section easy and actionable, try to plan out your life using the **WISER** model:

W - Why: Understand your why. Define it.
I - Introspection: Look inside and question. (*Self-awareness – coming up soon!*)
S - SMART Goals: Specific, measurable, attainable, relevant and time specific.
E - Execute: Do it. Don't just read it. Don't just write it. Action it.
R - Repeat: Like any habit that can change your life, make it a habit and repeat.

WISER is a simple approach to getting started on your own path to designing success. Your why provides the purpose, your SMART goals map out the plan, and repetition helps cement it as your new way of life. Each goal you set and achieve isn't just a step forward; it's an opportunity to see if you're moving closer to a life aligned with your deeper values, passions, and ideals. An effective reflective process keeps you grounded in your purpose, reminding you of the bigger picture as you go and keeping your motivation high.

One of the key strengths of the WISER model is its flexibility: it's not about rigid rules, but about creating a system that works for you. By continuously cycling through these steps, you can adapt to new challenges and opportunities while staying aligned with your long-term purpose. Whether you're using WISER to start a fitness journey, shift careers, or strengthen personal relationships, the model is designed to keep you focused, motivated, and evolving. It's not just a tool for achievement—it's a way to integrate self-reflection, structured planning, and consistent action into your daily life.

The other beauty of this kind of process is that it evolves with you. Life never stands still, and your goals and priorities may shift as you grow and have new experiences. By regularly looking back and reflecting on your why and your Ikigai, you stay connected to the bigger picture even as you navigate life's twists and turns. Whether you're rethinking a long-term career path or simply tweaking your daily routines, proper alignment between your goals and your whys ensures that your actions continue to move you toward a purposeful life.

These are the first, most fundamental tools to begin your success design journey. You might've already heard of some of these, but maybe not applied them to your own situation as thoroughly as you might. As you continue with this book, you'll find practical ways to use these tools to deepen your self-awareness, refine your why, and strengthen the habits you need to make this path your own. The journey may change as you gain new experiences, and your goals may shift, but returning to these three concepts – **your why, your goals, and your Ikigai** – ensures you're creating and designing success in a way that's sustainable, personal, and inspiring to you.

Strong Why, Strong Life, Strong Self.

Rashan Senanayake
@rashansenanayake
www.RashanSenanayake.com

PART 1 SUMMARY
These are the key takeaways in this section:

- **Why?** Always start with the why – it's the centre of our energy, our motivation, it's the start of everything. Understand the why and everything else falls into place.
- **Implement the 'Five Whys'** – This helps you get to the core of your foundational values, reasons and motivation behind any specific goal or challenge.
- **Make S.M.A.R.T (Specific, Measurable, Attainable, Relevant and Time Specific) Goals** – Being Specific is the start! Do this, no excuses – this brings your goal onto a sure-fire pathway towards making sure it can be achieved without veering off course.
- **Get W.I.S.E.R** - The formula for your success in achieving exactly what you want. The cornerstone of designing your success definition.

THE PERFECT LIBRARY DESIGN
Author's pick for these chapters

- **Start With Why** - Simon Sinek
- **SMART Goals : The Ultimate Goal Setting Guide** - Jacob Gudger
- **Find Your Why** - Peter Docker

Visit **www.rashansenanayak.com** for the full read list and more resources.

AUDIOBOOK + PODCAST
Extended discussions available on this section, exclusively on Audible.

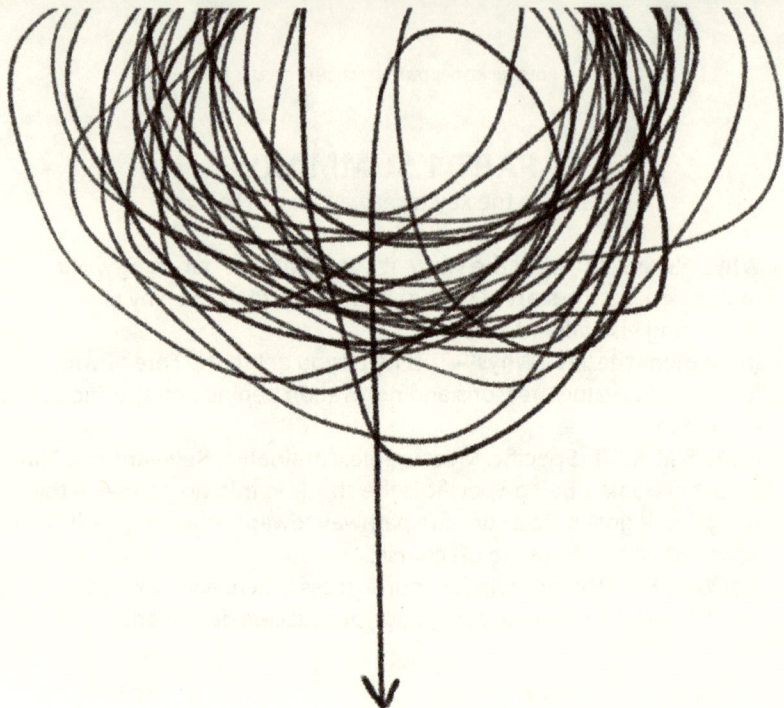

PART 2

SELF AWARNESS

PART 2: **SELF AWARENESS**

Self-awareness, by definition, means conscious knowledge of one's own character and feelings. In designing your success definition, self-awareness may seem like an obvious part of it. But you will be surprised how many go-getters overlook and lack self-awareness. This is why it's important to consciously focus on this skill when designing your success pathways. So, let's take a look.

Let me ask you a question – would you consider yourself a self-aware individual?

(You don't need to answer me, it was more a question for yourself.)

Let's first take a step back and understand the why behind the importance of being self-aware.

In the simplest way, developing self-awareness helps you learn, understand, and curate more about yourself and what you're capable of.

The ultimate result of this is... just awesome!

(It's almost like seeing the matrix in reality – beyond what's just visible on the surface)

When you understand yourself more *(become more self-aware)*, your self-esteem develops positively, which leads to increased confidence leading to a positive life, stronger relationships, and therefore your motivation and overall energy in your day to day life compounds exponentially. Your brain chemistry literally gets rewired towards a happy life. Being self-aware helps you to connect from deep within yourself and to stay true to your goals, values, and desires.

(Something to be aware of is that your self-awareness will be heavily related to your own values and beliefs, personal preferences, tendencies, circumstances and your own upbringing. Keep that in the back of your mind as you read through this book.)

One of the main outcomes from becoming self-aware is that you clearly understand your own strengths and limitations; you open up opportunities that just are not available otherwise *(or more accurately, you will not recognise them as opportunities)*. You will notice that your relationships in your life begin to become deeper, more honest, and more genuine – and most importantly, you stay true to yourself. You begin to see toxic relationships for what they are, you begin to see who and what adds value to your life. On top of all of this, a happy result is that, unconsciously, you will be perceived by others as a more attractive individual, simply because you are truly being who you are meant to be.

As a result, your mind becomes more sensitive to understanding other people's reactions to your actions – which leads to becoming a more secure individual while still being empathetic to others.

Can you now begin to see how important self-awareness is when you are designing your roadmap to a successful life?

If you don't, I recommend that you re-read the above section again!
If you do, then let's look at the actionable steps on how to be more self-aware.

Now, onto the good stuff!

5

CHAPTER 5: **WHO AM I?**

This is the million-dollar question!

Life is not about the number in your bank balance. It is not the car you drive or what other people think of you. It is about understanding yourself, staying true to yourself, and serving and adding value to others.

(Things got a bit philosophical there, didn't they?)

Answering this question *(or attempting to answer this question)* is step one in gaining more self-awareness. However, keep in mind that this is an ongoing question. As you go through this process, revisiting this question over and over again is very important – simply because it keeps things in check and consistently allows you to design yourself along the way. After all, change is inevitable as we journey through life.

Answering this question is much harder *(and slower)* than you think. But the good thing is that you have already begun this journey and would've already achieved a certain level of self-awareness – otherwise you would not have made the conscious decision to read this book!

So, how do you answer this question? Well, there are a series of ongoing actions you can take that will develop your self-awareness.

1. Self-Talk!

No… this does not mean sit in a corner and talk to yourself and make your loved ones worry about your mental health. Doing that may actually be a negative action.

No! Not at all.

What this term refers to is the process of internal reflection, in the form of a dialogue. It is about following the Five Whys rules, internally. It is about asking yourself the right questions to understand the cause and effect of a feeling, thought, reaction, or mindset.

For example: *Kelly, a 24-year-old Marketing Executive, had her Director cut her off during her client presentation very rudely, which affected the entire end result. She was not able to deliver the product solution she had tirelessly worked on – he ultimately stole her thunder and all the credit. As a result, Kelly is now feeling very angry and frustrated towards her Director and is reactively entertaining the thought process of quitting because she feels that this company has nothing to offer her career under this bad leadership.*

Activating self-talk in this scenario would create an internal dialogue. Kelly could ask herself a series of questions and search for answers intrinsically:

- *Why am I feeling this way? I am frustrated because I worked hard on the presentation looking to lead this project and get promoted – but he just cut me off and ruined the presentation and stole all the credit. Now I have no leverage to apply for that promotion.*
- *Why? Because I want…*
- *Why? Because I am thinking of myself…*
- *Why? Because I am reacting selfishly…*
- *Why? Because of my own desires and perhaps ego?…*

This allows Kelly to firstly understand her own standpoint. Understand and accept her emotions, while using logic to reason and guide the thought process. Now she is **ready** to take the next step.

(I have emphasised the word 'ready'. This is done intentionally to emphasise the importance of understanding your own perspective first, before you can objectively empathise or sympathise with another person.)

- *Why did he react that way to me? Because he is a rude prick! But normally he is a nice person – it's confusing!*
- *Why did he react that way today? Because he's stressed?*
- *Why would he be stressed though? Because without this project the company*

may risk losing a lot of staff and restructuring.

• *So why did he really cut me off? Because he wanted to take control of the project and add his value into the client's presentation in his own way and make sure it came through. Afterall, the client is engaged now – teamwork?*

So, it was not because I did a bad job... I should speak to him about helping him to make sure we land the next client we are working on. I will ask if he is okay and what I can do to help them.

• *Why? Because that is the best thing I can do now, and it is in my control. If he says no, then no worries – I have done everything I can and given everything I have.*

Always look at taking action on affecting things that ARE actually within your control, without worrying about what is not in your control – this includes things that you perceive to be within your control. For example: Kelly expecting her director to apologise and then praise her!

The result of that story: Kelly got promoted because she helped the company land the next client and lighten his workload by acting in higher duties. Following the project, Kelly was recognised as a forward thinker, putting the company's needs first, over her own. She was seen as a team player!

This is of course, an example only. However, you can see how after a few minutes *(or seconds after it becomes a habit)* of self-talk, the reactive actions *(quitting her job)* based on her own needs and ego were transformed into a selfless act, which resulted in the promotion and a positive result.

If internally reflecting seems difficult, then write it down!
Self-talk! In the words of our friends at Nike: "Just do it" – it works.

66

"Just Do It."

Nike
(Company Slogan)

2. 7th Sense

Next is to follow step 1 – but using all of your senses. Your ability to do this is your 7th sense: your sharpened intuition and ability to read others and empathise.

Your senses can provide you with a large amount of insights into your own and other peoples' feelings, reactions, body language, and situations in general. Without our senses, we may misunderstand a situation due to incorrect filters and react emotionally in self-defence and self-interest. Afterall, it is human nature to do so! So, this is about going against the grain and rewiring your brain to unlock hidden potential.

For example, a frown doesn't always mean that someone is angry. Using your senses and self-talk can allow you to identify that situation as someone just thinking hard or as a person with a RBF *(Resting Bitch Face – like one of my closest architecture friends with a solid beard!)*.

In practice, the next time you feel that someone is judging you or has made you feel bad/good about yourself, take a step back and use your 7th sense and self-talk to understand the actual reality of the situation, despite what your internal voice or reaction may be.

This process becomes quicker and quicker the more it is practised.

3. Listen to your feelings!

This may sound like the (second) most corny statement in the world. But do yourself a favour and read on before reacting.

This is the last piece of the puzzle to gaining more self-awareness and answering that million-dollar question: *"Who am I?"*

Listening to your feelings can be a very hard thing to do, especially if you are not used to it or generally think of yourself as a masculine individual who just doesn't like to think about feelings deeply.

However, the reality is that all our feelings are spontaneous, and emotional responses are a result of the situation. Similar to the 7th sense, our feelings are a huge indication and a great source of information about ourselves, and are a valuable tool should we choose to tune into them.

Usually our emotions manifest through some sort of a physical reaction, for example:

- A warm feeling in your face might mean you're embarrassed or shy.
- The feeling of butterflies in your stomach can mean you're nervous or excited.
- Clenching your teeth might mean you're angry or stressed.

In practice, tune into physical signs that will indicate how you're feeling. By doing so, you will gain insight to your feelings and therefore understand yourself more clearly.

Fact: If you can develop this skill, it can allow you to understand your physiological movements and reactions to enforce your wellbeing.

(What in the world does that mean? Ask me.)

Self-awareness is the foundation to any success map.

Rashan Senanayake
@rashansenanayake
www.RashanSenanayake.com

CHAPTER SUMMARY: SELF AWARENESS
These are the key takeaways in this section:

- **Self-awareness is a practice** – it's not a switch that can be turned on and off. It is a lifetime learning process and practice. So, adopt a growth mindset and practice, practice, practice.
- **Understand who you are** – Ask yourself *"Who am I?"* This is the core question that you will constantly revisit at each point in your life's journey. This way, you can learn to take action that is true to yourself, true to who you are.
- **Step 1: Self Talk** – Self reflecting allows you to gain more insight into who you are and understand the core reasoning behind anything and everything. Execute this in combination with the learnings from the previous chapter and follow the Five Whys rule.
- **Step 2: Engage your 7th Sense** – This is where you are able to reflect on yourself from the third person and understand what is happening, what the why is without any bias to yourself – a key ingredient in designing your definition of success.
- **Step 3: Listen to your feelings** – Learn to hear them, accept them, and understand the results – whether physiological or psychological, it all feeds into your self-awareness.

THE PERFECT LIBRARY DESIGN
Author's pick for this chapter

- **Think and Grow Rich** - Napoleon Hill
- **Get Out of Your Own Way: Overcoming Self-Defeating Behaviour** - Mark Soulston & Phillip Goldberg
- **Working with Emotional Intelligence** - Daniel Goleman

Visit **www.rashansenanayak.com** for the full read list and more resources.

AUDIOBOOK + PODCAST
Extended discussions available on this section, exclusively on Audible.

6

CHAPTER 6: **PERSONALITY** ——————————

Perfect! Now that you are aware of how to answer, *"Who am I?"* let's look at understanding your own personality type. This is important for two main reasons:

1. Understanding yourself in a standard of measure.
2. Gaining the ability to understand others.

The easiest method to understand your personality is by taking a personality test. However, there are over 30 different types of personality tests that you can take. So, feel free if you wish.

But for the sake of understanding yourself and the different types of personalities *(and to save you a lot of time!)* the D.I.S.C profiling personality test is great.

This is one of the most popular personality tests that can be taken online. It is a behaviour assessment tool based on the DISC theory of psychologist William Moulton Marston, which centres on four different behavioural traits:

- **Dominance (D)**
- **Influence (I)**
- **Conscientious (C)**
- **Steadiness (S)**

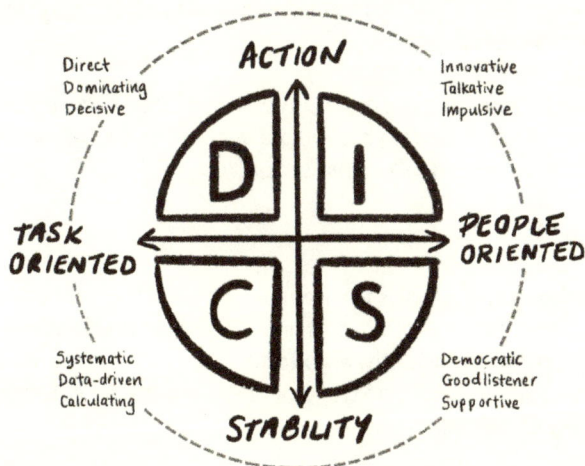

TIME TO TAKE ACTION!

Check out the downloadable resources for this section
at www.rashansenanayake.com

So, let's break down the various profile types:

- **Dominance (D)**

As the word describes, they are the direct, decisive types. D-personality types would always try to take charge and lead rather than follow and are suited more towards the leadership and management positions. They have a high level of self-confidence, are relatively high risk takers, and problem solvers which positions them as a leader who others look for decisions and directions from. Dominant personality types are also self-starters with a higher tendency for intrinsic motivation *(more on this in the next section)*.

On the flip side, this personality type can very easily overstep authority because they see themselves as the leader. Which can lead to arguments without care or reasoning for others. They will shy away from routines and dislike repetition and ignore details – even if it's important! Stemming from their (potential) overconfidence, they can tend to attempt too many things at one time, looking for fast results.

D-types can have a massive insecurity and fear of being taken advantage of – this leads to their lack of trust in others. However, the heavy motivation for the D-type personality is mainly in new challenges and taking risks, being free from routine and everyday tasks.

(Raise your hand if you think you are a D-type personality! If you actually raised your hand, I've got bad news for you: you are definitely not a D-type, because they wouldn't want to be led and follow instructions!)

- **Influence (I)**

In a nutshell, the I-personality is the people person of the group. They are the centre of attention, enthusiastic, optimistic; they can be persuasive, talkative, impulsive, and, most importantly, emotional. They inherently are a very trustworthy personality type and genuinely enjoy working collaboratively in teams and around people.

In contrast, this personality is likely not the best at detailed work as they are more driven by people and popularity than results. As they are very much self-centred and highly expressive, they can be bad at listening and give the impression of always waiting to speak, rather than listening intently and being present.

The I-type's greatest fear is rejection, but they are highly motivated by popularity, praise, and acceptance. They always seek a friendly environment and therefore may avoid tough situations, reducing their grit.

(Did you read this description and think you are an I-type? Well if you are, you would've most likely said it out loud and shared the news with your family or friends already!)

- **Steadiness (S)**

S-personality types are the easiest people to work with. They are identified as being steady *(as the name indicates)* but predictable. They are even-tempered, friendly and sympathetic with others and are very generous with loved ones. They are also the best listeners of the group that highly value their close personal relationships, which can potentially lead them to be possessive.

Their weakness lies in resistance to change and taking a long time to adjust to anything imparted on them. They can potentially hold grudges for a long time, and are sensitive to criticism as well. Some S-types can find it difficult to establish priorities for themselves.

Their biggest fear lies in the loss of security while being highly driven by the recognition of their loyalty and dependability. They enjoy a routine lifestyle with security and safety, with few changes.

(A Golden Retriever is essentially an I-Type + S-Type or 'IS'. Did you associate yourself with being an S-Type? Let's keep going – and thanks for being a team player.)

- **Conscientious (C)**

The C-personality type are the analysts in the group. They are very accurate, precise, detail-oriented, and conscientious. These mainly left brained individuals are driven by analytical and systematic thinking, whilst making decisions very carefully after thorough research and information overload. They always strive to be the best and have very high standards for not only themselves, but others as well. C-types can also be highly creative individuals, stemming from their nature to be great problem solvers, focusing on the details that most others will choose to ignore.

On the other side, C-types are heavily bound by procedures and methods and can get bogged down in detail too much, which prevents them from making decisions. They are a more submissive personality type that would prefer to give in rather than argue.

Being very sensitive, C-types greatest fear lies in criticism. While they are driven and motivated by a high standard of quality, introverted tendencies and detailed tasks with an organised information.

(Did you analyse every type carefully and break down the details of each personality type? Welcome to the C-club!)

So, let's do the test and find out your type in more detail: time to take action!

1.   Google 'DISC Profile Test' and pick one.
2.   Then share the results with your family and friends.
3.   Try to guess your family and friends' profile types.
4.   Ask them to take the test and see how accurate you are!

One thing I must highlight at this point is that we have ALL of these traits in some way or form. This is why when you read through each type it may feel confusing identifying which type suits your personality. But going through this process allows you to understand which two types are the strongest. For example, you may be a DI (Dominant and Influence) or CD (Conscientious and Dominant) or SI (Steady and Influence). Regardless, we all have one strong type, with a secondary type. The DISC profiling test is designed to allow you to understand it as such.

The author of this book is a **'DI' Dominance** coupled with **Influence**.

Do you feel as though you now have more clarity about who you are and can be more self-aware?

If you don't, then put a bookmark on this page, put this book down and spend more time on self-reflection and study.

If you do, then achievement unlocked!

> Don't ever let your surroundings
> dictate your personality.
>
> Always let your personality define your
> surroundings and be true to yourself.

Rashan Senanayake
@rashansenanayake
www.RashanSenanayake.com

CHAPTER SUMMARY: PERSONALITY

These are the key takeaways in this section:

- **There are many personality tests** – Select one and try to understand more about your personality.
- **We have all traits** – Every personality trait and characteristic is found within our own personality. But it varies on a scale allowing some traits to be stronger than the others.
- **One is not better than the other** – Each personality type has their own pros and cons, strengths and weaknesses. Understanding your own traits and harnessing them is the key.
- **Your personality traits can make you more suitable for a certain job over others** – It comes with your personality. Naturally you will be more suitable to certain jobs and roles over others. For example, a D-Dominant personality will be more successful at a leadership or management role.

THE PERFECT LIBRARY DESIGN

Author's pick for this chapter

- **Do What You Are** - Paul D. Tieger, Barbara Barron & Kelly Tieger
- **The Personality Brokers: The Strange History of Myers-Briggs and the Birth of Personality Testing** - Merve Emre
- **How to Win Friends and Influence People** - Dale Carnegie

---

Visit **www.rashansenanayak.com** for the full read list and more resources.

AUDIOBOOK + PODCAST

Extended discussions available on this section, exclusively on Audible.

7

CHAPTER 7: **MOTIVATION**

Since your motivation to keep reading is at a high at the moment, let's cut to the good stuff.

Scientifically speaking, motivation is your general willingness to move towards a certain task, goal, or action. It is the forces (*or neurological pulses*) that tell us to take action.

In my experience, motivation is extremely fickle. It is inconsistent and not reliable. It is a balancing act. It is about priorities. Ultimately, it is a game.

(Before we get into the details, I must say that motivation is something that varies from person to person. Everything that has led you up to this very moment of reading this page has and can influence your motivation differently towards different tasks, actions, and goals. Therefore, is it important to build on the first chapters of this book and tailor your learnings to your life)

We all have a tipping point where the consequences of not taking action on something becomes greater than the pain (or pleasure) of taking action. This is where suddenly we have all the motivation in the world to get things done! At this point, it becomes easier to take action and change, ultimately shedding away all the excuses and obstacles to reach the goal – do or die.

When you have a date next week and you want to look your best, it becomes easier to go to the gym every day and lift those heavy weights, than to sit on the couch and binge watch Netflix, Stan, Disney+, whatever you prefer!

When you have to pass that particular unit to graduate, and the submission date is in forty-eight hours, it becomes easier to begin that project you have been putting off than to procrastinate and waste hours on Facebook *(reading 'useful' articles)*, trying to feel productive.

Usually this tipping point is tied to a strong emotion attached to a personal effect. When emotions such as physical pain or pleasure, fear of something, or happiness plays its role, we tend to have more motivation and can easily act.

Let's take a look at Jenny.

(We all know a Jenny!)

Jenny has been hating attending her history subject at university. But it's now the last week and her final examination to pass the entire subject is in one week. She hasn't had any motivation to go to class, listen to lectures, or even pick up the textbook! She barely passed the two in-class quizzes *(without studying - but only because she's a bright case!)*.

One week out, she came to the realisation that if she fails this unit, she will have to repeat the class next year and delay her graduation by yet another year. If that happens, then she cannot have her gap year and travel to Europe, before she enters the workforce.

This is the tipping point *(or a 'catalyst cause')* where Jenny's pain of not taking action clearly outweighs her hate and lack of interest in the subject. In the following week leading up to her exam, she will have all the motivation, clear focus and a strong why to GET IT DONE!

(Are you beginning to see how the previous chapters are connecting with your motivation? They are all interrelated and these chapters were organised by design.)

As you can see, motivation is driven and heavily influenced by our emotions. Emotions are tied to a cause and effect, pain or gain for yourself – your why. To cross this mental threshold, next we need to be able to understand a few things:

1.	The different types of motivation; and,
2.	how to action them.

We can then answer the age-old question of how to consistently be motivated regardless of your circumstances, even though you might not feel like it and have self-declared yourself to be a "Procrastination Queen/King".

Types of Motivation

While you are reading this section, try to self-reflect, guestimate and understand which characteristics best describe *you*.

As you already know, motivation is driven from emotions, which drives our behavioural patterns. Psychologists have proposed different ways of thinking about motivational factors, including one particular method that relates to looking at whether motivation arises externally (extrinsic) or internally (intrinsic) from the individual.

While both types of motivation are important and can be utilised well, research has proven that intrinsic motivation and extrinsic motivation can have a whole variety of different effects on our actions, especially in how people pursue their own goals. This is why it is crucial to gain clarity and to understand each one and how they work. Let's get straight into it!

Extrinsic Motivation

This is where we are motivated to behave, engage with, or take action in an activity to earn a (usually tangible) reward, or avoid punishment – external to our self.

Examples of various extrinsic motivations are:
- Studying because you have to pass an exam or get good grades.
- Cleaning your room to avoid a scolding or receive an allowance.
- Playing sports for an award.
- Working hard at your job for the cash only.
- A promotion.
- To receive validation or praise from others.

Each time, the motivation is driven by the desire or fear to gain or avoid (respectively) the external outcome. At these points, we are engaging in the activity and behaving not because we enjoy it or for satisfaction, but for some type of return on investment.

Intrinsic Motivation

This is where we are motivated to behave, engage with, or take action in an activity because it is personally rewarding – essentially, performing an activity for its own internal merits.

Examples of various intrinsic motivations are:
- Studying because the subject is interesting to you.
- Cleaning your room, because you like your surroundings to be neat and tidy.
- Playing sport for the enjoyment and satisfaction of competing.
- Working hard at your job because it is fulfilling and/or helps others.
- Working on your health for your own happiness.

In these scenarios, you are motivated by an internal desire, fulfilment, or satisfaction.

(Which is the better type of motivation?)

Well, the primary difference between the two types is simply the origin of the thought process – mindset.

Research has proven over and over again that a large external behaviour can reduce the intrinsic motivation within us through a psychological phenomenon called the Over Justification Effect. A study shows that children who were rewarded for playing with a toy they had already expressed interest in playing became less interested in it and abandoned it quickly after they have been exposed to a more attractive external reward – a brand new toy that is battery powered.

(Kids! Am I right? Well, we all do it too.)

I am not suggesting that extrinsic motivation is the bad one here – definitely not! It can be highly beneficial in particular scenarios. Especially in a context where you find the task unpleasant, external rewards may feel as though they are the only way to get things over the line.

External rewards can be used to encourage extrinsic motivation, to help boost interest and drive the actions of a person that originally may not have had any interest to begin with. For example, to persuade someone to acquire a new skill, or to study a subject that they are unaware of but could be beneficial to them in the long run. Following which (based on other factors as well), the individual may then become more intrinsically motivated to pursue that activity for their internal satisfaction and gratification. Additionally, it can be used as a great source of feedback at schools and universities as a guidance system for students to reinforce an achieved standard. This can in turn increase intrinsic motivation in studying a certain subject and in pursuing a career long term.

But be careful! You should not try to extrinsically motivate an already intrinsically motivated person. This can make the situation that was already rewarding to them seem more like work and transform it into an unpleasant task or situation.

Coming back to answer that question of *"which is the better one?"*, through my own experience and in my opinion, it is intrinsic motivation.

(Why?)

Well… let me share a quick story! As you already might be aware, starting a company is no easy feat, let alone two companies in my case. Prior to the current companies in operation, I co-founded and operated an Events Management company, which was later dissolved for a multitude of reasons. However, one of the primary reasons was that its success was hinged on my motivation – to be more specific, the extrinsic motivation was the financial reward. There was no connection to the actual work or value towards our clients, it was simply profit driven. Within less than a year this feat became very dry and an empty work-life relationship affected all our team members – which ultimately led to a failed chapter.

(Failed, but many lessons learned!)

One of the personal reasons this company failed was that the profit made from this company hinged on the sale and consumption of alcohol!

(By the way – since I haven't mentioned it already – I do not consume any alcohol. It is not part of my life and nor is it something that I find any value in.)

(But why!?)

(Many, many reasons! Ask me why when you ask to get this book signed)

Once this was pointed out to me, I tried to justify my reasoning by saying *"Well, we are not making money from alcohol at all! The club/event/bar/venue is doing that… not us!"* But in reality, I was just lying to myself. These types of events were driven mainly by the consumption of alcohol.

(Don't get me wrong! There is nothing wrong in enjoying a drink, or with the consumption of alcohol. It just simply does not align with my own personal values. Some of the best friends are the biggest scotch/beer drinkers ever to roam planet Earth!).

However, even after most of the other team members had left the company – I kept experimenting with different ideas to see if it can be done by creating value for people – without the involvement of alcohol. We did talent unveilings, charity/not-for-profit work, and various cultural events. But if you didn't guess it already, it was A LOT OF WORK, and very little commercial gain equals a failed company.

So, the motivation that was hinged on this extrinsic chase for profit was quickly thrown out the window, after realising its clash with my own morals. Therefore, it could (and would) never work!

But the learned lessons from this experience are carried forward into today, in helping start-ups and other entrepreneurs achieve their own success through one of my current companies. It is more profitable and aligns well with my morality, skill sets, and passion for design.

Coming back to the question above: *"Which motivation type is better?"* Well, based on my experience and research, I would personally prefer and rely on cultivating intrinsic motivation over extrinsic motivation any day of the week!

(Why?)
(Good Question!)

Well, a number of factors, such as:
• Being in control of your own energy and consequently, your resulting actions.
• Purpose and satisfaction achieved through your own actions.
• Increased self-esteem and self-worth through the actions based on intrinsic motivation.

Ultimately a more rewarding lifestyle and life!

This can then lead to more intrinsically motivated goals, which results in your life's work also becoming your passion.

Well, when that happens… there is no stopping you!

It is a beautiful life – a life that most cannot understand, until they have experienced it themselves.

"

Success is not the key to happiness.
Happiness is the key to success.

If you love what you are doing,
you will be successful.

Albert Schweitzer
Theologian, Organist, Writer, Humanitarian, Philosopher and Physician

Motivation as a 'switch'

Reading this book is all well and great… but it's no use if you don't know HOW to use it in your day to day life.

Speaking from personal experience, I follow a very specific process to control my motivators. Here is the roadmap to what I do to control my motivation and to use it as a switch, to turn it ON or OFF as I desire. This is much easier said than done, so don't take this lightly!

(Hint: the secret lies in your habits.)

For the time being, let me walk you through how to get motivated, even when you *"don't feel like it"*, and have control over when you want to turn it on or off.

(It is perfectly timed that I am writing this part, while I am sitting at QUT until my next meeting at 5.45pm. I am exhausted after travelling interstate for the past three days and only returning close to midnight last night. Then completing client work and teaching my 4th years for six straight hours. I have zero motivation due to low energy and it has resulted in the lack of any type of motivation. However, that won't stop me from writing this part, because my why is clear, my goals are focused and therefore I can switch ON my motivation as required.)

(How?)

Well, it all comes down to:
1.   Acting before thinking *(I will explain this more)*.
2.   Making it a continous habit.

If you study how high performance and successful individuals function – individuals such as professional athletes, world renowned speakers, the biggest entrepreneurs of the world, CEOs and even high achieving students – it is all based around the steps leading up to this point and making it a habit (hence why the last chapter of this book discusses habits).

Almost every high performing individual has a tailored morning routine, a fitness and health routine, a consistent schedule for anything in their life. What this does is that it takes motivation (in its default mode) out of the equation, and transforms it into a consistent and dependable pattern. It becomes a habit.

After a while, through consistent application, our brain then begins to identify tasks that usually require motivation as routine, and therefore encounter less resistance from your brain. In other words, things just happen and your physiological reaction is to find and muster the energy required to work through your routine habits. This is however a double-edged sword – the same practice applies to bad habits (more on this in Chapter 22).

Let me pause here for a few seconds and let you digest that above section.

Really let that sink in…

Keep reading it until you can repeat it back to yourself. Keep reading it until it begins to make sense…

…

…

…

(Breathe. Think.) Alright! Let's continue.

Because your brain is seeing something as routine, you begin to take action, actioning tasks on autopilot and begin to act before thinking. Why is this? Your brain requires energy to make decisions, to think, to analyse – even small decisions such as *"what should I wear today?"* Therefore, when it is a habit, a routine, the conserved energy can be utilised to take action on tasks required.

Now it is time to address the most important question on motivation: *"How can you have your motivation as a switch which can be turned on and off?"*

Let's look at some very easy ways (or triggers) for getting yourself into building the mindset to harness motivation as a switch:

To exercise more consistently: Design an easy routine for you that leads to exercise. The result: you start without thinking and all of a sudden you are in the middle of your workout. The resistance to working out is gone. Here are some easy triggers:

- Listen to your workout playlist
- Prepare your protein drinks/supplements
- Watch a snippet of your favourite inspirational movie
- Get in the car
- Change into your gym outfit

To be more creative: Follow a specific set of tasks before you write, paint, design, sing etc. The result: you begin to feel inspired to work on your creative tasks. Here some easy triggers:

- Look on Pinterest for work that inspires your creative brain
- Listen to music that you like
- Play with your pet and come back to your work
- Listen to a podcast that inspires you
- Watch a YouTube video on your favourite designer

Avoid stress/anxiety/depression: Create a quick 3-5 minute routine to be used when you begin to feel stressed, which firstly acknowledges your stress, and secondly changes your physiological reactions to enable your body to better manage this overwhelm. For example, try a 2 minute square breathing exercise to slow your heart rate, that will regulate your blood flow and decrease your stress. Here are some other useful tips:

- Combine this with gratitude practice.
- Speak to a loved one about a different topic.
- Reflect on what you have already achieved in your life.

Sleep better: Follow a specific routine before getting into bed. For example: set your alarm, check the weather, prepare your clothes/items for tomorrow, brush teeth/shower, etc. The result: your mind will automatically re-adjust and expect sleep while you go through that process. This will result in better sleep. Here are some more useful tips:

- Give yourself a screen break.
- Do some light stretches to help get better blood flow.
- Meditate to calm your mind and body.

These are what's called 'pre-game routines' that elite athletes follow before every game, without missing a step. It provides a simple yet effective way for your mind to initiate, focus, and engage your behaviour. It gives you the keys to unlocking the door to summon the energy required for important work and decision making: *"What should I do first?" "When should I start?" "How should I do this?"* Most people never move forward because they cannot get past these simple, yet daunting questions. By establishing routines, your behaviours become easy and automatic, so you can complete the action when something becomes challenging.

Ultimately you can then design your own habits (*see chapter 22*) to achieve almost anything you want – you can do this consistently and set yourself up for success.

> **Make a choice. Just decide.**
> **What it's gonna be, who you're gonna be,**
> **how you're gonna do it.**
> **Just decide.**

Will Smith

Actor, Producer, Rapper, Songwriter and much more

CHAPTER SUMMARY: MOTIVATION
Let me outline the 80/20 version of the motivation section:

- **Motivation is your energy output** – It is your general willingness to carry out activities that relate to various parts of your life. Anything from work, to play, to study, etc.
- **There are two types of motivation: intrinsic and extrinsic** – Both have positive and negative attributes that can be workable.
- **Intrinsic motivation** – Refers to the type of motivation that drives you for your own internal rewards. For example, your own happiness, fulfilment, and purpose.
- **Extrinsic motivation** – Refers to the type of motivation that drives you based on external rewards. For example, status, fame, money, or material wealth.
- **Create positive habits** – So you require less motivational energy to carry out good practice.
- **Use motivation as a switch** – Learn how to turn your motivation on and off at your will, based on a systematic approach derived from heightened self-awareness.
- **Motivation as a tool** – Learn to utilise your motivation as a part of your tool kit for defining your own definition of success.

THE PERFECT LIBRARY DESIGN
Author's pick for this chapter

- **7 Habits of Highly Effective People** - Stephen R . Covey
- **The Power of Positive Thinking** - Norman Vincent Peale
- **Power of Now** - Eckhart Tolle

Visit **www.rashansenanayak.com** for the full read list and more resources.

AUDIOBOOK + PODCAST
Extended discussions available on this section, exclusively on Audible.

8

CHAPTER 8: **LEARNING STYLES** —————————

Now that you have gained a fair bit of insight into yourself, let's build on this. To be able to design your definition of a successful life, another piece of the masterpiece *(that is you)* is to understand how we learn, grow, and absorb information. There are many different types of learning styles, and most of us are a combination of many. However, once you know which type of learning style best suits you, you will be able to double down on your strengths and harness its power to level up!

So, let's take a look at the different types of learning styles:

- **Visual** (Spatial): prefer seeing pictures, images, and various spatial instructions.
- **Aural** (Auditory): prefer using sounds and other audio to learn.
- **Verbal** (Linguistic): prefer using spoken words, usually in speech and writing.
- **Physical** (Kinesthetic): prefer using your body, hands and sense of touch/feel.
- **Logical** (Mathematical): prefer using logic, reasoning, and systems.
- **Social** (interpersonal): prefer to learn in groups or with other people.
- **Solitary** (intrapersonal): prefer to work alone and use self-study.

Personally speaking, when absorbing information, I would much rather listen to an audiobook or a podcast over reading the physical book. The information enters in my mind easier *(through active listening techniques)* and I will retain the content for a much longer time period. Therefore, I am more 'aural' at absorbing new information.

This is combined with visual elements that allow me to develop a photographic memory over time *(yes, it can be a learned skill!)*. This is very useful when trying to recall and retain existing information, such as numbers, textbook pages, designs, locations, pictures, or visual representations. I will remember a person's face easily and recall where I met them, because of the visual representation.

These are just a few examples of how it has benefitted my day to day activities. But something we must be aware of is that we all possess every single learning style. It is a matter of understanding what works best for yourself and your life – by design.

So, ask yourself:

Which method allows me to remember things better?

Which method allows me to absorb new information quicker?

Which allows me to be more present and retain/recall memories?

(Is it visual, aural, kinaesthetic, etc.)

Test out each method over a few weeks and iterate your learning style. You may find that it is a combination of a few different learning styles. Or you lean towards one certain type.

There is no right or wrong – but you become a more self-aware person and begin to skyrocket your learning – a crucial step in designing your definition of success.

Vertical & Horizontal Learning

Once you understand your learning style(s), you can then take things to the next level. Learning is not 1-dimensional. It is not even 2-dimensional. If you are to transcend your being and design your life, you must embrace and view learning to be 3-dimensional.

What does this mean? Well, learning about your learning styles will instil a

level of mindful self-awareness and allow you to develop your skills on any application as you need to. To help you absorb, consume, and understand knowledge, faster and more productively. However, what you learn and how you grow as an individual is also a learning style.
There are two main categories for this:

- **Horizontal Learning**
- **Vertical Learning**

(Never heard of them? Good!)

Discussed in this chapter so far are all the different types of learning styles, which refer to horizontal learnings. The fact is, you may already be quite good at horizontal learning, because this is what is taught to us from a very young age. A good example is learning to drive a car. When you were incompetent – just starting out – you were mindful and alert to every action involved in driving. The pedal, the gear stick, the steering, everything on the road, your instructor. However, once you master this more and more through practice, you gradually become consciously competent. This then allows you to carry out the actions required consciously, yet confidently. From this point on, fast forward a few years of driving and you are now unconsciously competent. Which means that getting in the car and driving, road rules, the pedal, steering, gear shift, etc. are all things that automatically happen, while you are able to continue a conversation with the fellow passengers.

Some of us take this too far by even texting while driving and this is what leads to more human error! We become so confident in our unconscious competency that we begin taking risks.

But that's a topic for another day.

Horizontal learning has four stages in acquiring any skill:

- **Unconsciously incompetent** – you don't even know you can't do something.
- **Consciously incompetent** – you know you are bad at something but cannot perform what is required.
- **Consciously competent** – you know you are good at something and can perform what's required.
- **Unconsciously competent** – you now don't even know your skills and are on autopilot, performing what is required.

That is horizontal learning. Learning a skill. Whether it's driving a car, riding a bike, learning how to walk, coding on a computer, engineering, medicine… or any other skill set. This is called horizontal because we have a logical sequence of learning, to move from one knowledge step to the next, with the skills gradually becoming more complex. For example, starting off as an apprentice/graduate and becoming a master or a director (in a professional context).

All the various learning styles we have discussed earlier in this chapter essentially help you absorb the required knowledge within horizontal learning. Our education system is built to create and facilitate various horizontal learning opportunities for various skill sets to allow us to fit into the workplace. However, this is something that evolves and changes constantly – and in this new era, it can be very difficult to keep up!

(So, what is vertical learning?)

Now you are talking! This is the right question, and this is what sets you apart and helps you design your own definition of success. This is what the 1% do to take their horizontal learnings to the next level.

Vertical learning is your 'vertical development' over the course of your lifetime. Through the various stages of consciousness. It's the *(awesome)* ability to hold more and more complexity, to increasingly add more perspective to your awareness and develop emotional intelligence, resilience, and mindfulness *(all items discussed later in this book)*.

Have you felt you have outgrown a certain job, relationship, or even a hobby or interest? These things don't seem to interest you anymore, and you feel there is more out there, more to discover, more range, more complexity, more value, more purpose, more happiness.

Of course you have! You don't still play with the same toys you had when you were five years old, or even think the same way anymore. You don't crawl everywhere, you now walk, run, ride, or even drive to where you want to go to. This is the evolution of vertical (physical) learning. Similarly – as you wouldn't think the same way as when you were five years old – we increase our capability to reflect, to become more self-aware and evolve mindfully. Vertical learning is transformative and allows us to increase our capacity to hold and embody more consciousness. An open heart, an open mind, can elevate us into a capacity of higher emotional intelligence and resilience.

This is also called wisdom.

However, when you intentionally instil vertical learning techniques, it allows you to transcend faster and design your life towards your own definition of success.

Imagine yourself – more accurately, your development – as an apartment building. One that has more levels than you are even aware of at this point.

When you are on the ground level, your vision is bound by the property fence and the immediate surroundings. All you can see is what is inside the fence. This is the extent of your vision. Just over the fence, you can see glimpses of the surrounding environment – but not enough detail to grasp a full picture. Developing yourself further, you will move on up to level one/two/three. At this level you can now see everything inside your property fence, and the details of the immediate environment. You have a clear vision of the surrounding buildings, trees, and roads, and you begin to see over the smaller buildings to see further out as well. All of a sudden, the small environment inside the property fence is beginning to seem small and insignificant. But you are still attached to it. However, now having a taste for vertical learning, you begin building and transcending further. Moving on to level five/six/seven – you can now see well over all the surrounding buildings. Almost have a full vision of the entire block and the neighbouring blocks and can begin to see far out! You are now beginning to lose sight of what was inside your property fence. Simply because your vision is now so broad and encompasses a bigger world.

Eventually you will keep building higher and higher and come to a point where you can see so far out over your city and maybe even the ocean – far and wide! The insufficient issues that were once held within your property fence no longer faze you. You see the bigger picture, a bigger world, more complexity and possess a higher emotional intelligence – all whilst being able to take in much more than when you were originally on ground level.

So keep building vertically. Transcend.

(Is one better than the other?)

That is a valid question – and the answer is a bit more complicated than simply choosing one over the other. Simply put, we need both horizontal and vertical learning and development – simultaneously. However, vertical development is very rarely taught in the traditional context – or even encouraged. Although this is now changing. Regardless, it is something that can be part of your self-education and the simple fact that you are reading this at this very moment means that you are on the journey towards your vertical learning and development. Vertical learning is essential for any leadership context – whether in a professional or personal context.

"

Vertical learning not only upgrades a leader's operating system; it requires their hardware and expands their leadership competency and capacity. It literally alters brain functioning and recreates a leader's world view.

Barrett C. Brow

Ph.D. The Future of Leadership for Conscious Capitalism

Vertical learning involves exactly what makes great leaders, change makers, creative entrepreneurs, athletes, or anyone we may consider to be successful: the capacity for perspective-taking, for showing care and concern (empathy), for embracing diversity with an open heart and mind (broad vision), for maintaining high states of mindful action, overcoming adversity at all costs (resilience), intentional practice, discipline, and choosing to live a life geared with purpose – living by design, not by default.

Now, you are probably wondering if I am going to shortcut your success and give you the key to all of this. Well you are absolutely right! I am about to tell you exactly how you can achieve the same and know exactly how to climb up the vertical development ladder.

Are you ready?

Are you sure?

Good.

One word: **Practise**.

Three words: **Practise self-awareness**.

Consistent, deliberate and disciplined practice with progressively increasing complex awareness of yourself (me), your context (us) and the world (all encompassing).

Of course, the starting point is yourself (your why).

TIME TO TAKE ACTION!

Check out the downloadable resources for this section
at www.rashansenanayake.com

Learning is a journey, not a destination.

Rashan Senanayake
@rashansenanayake
www.RashanSenanayake.com

`CHAPTER SUMMARY: LEARNING STYLES
Short summary, for a short section:

- **There are many different learning styles** – Everything from aural, taste, kinesthetic, verbal, physical – just to name a few.
- **The key is to learn how you learn** – Ask yourself, *"What method allows me to remember things better? "What method allows me to absorb new information quicker?"* Then you can double down on what works best for you.
- **Understand about your horizontal learning stages** – Develop self-awareness to progress your horizontal learning in any context, as required. Be aware of it while it's happening and deliberately walk through the stages.
- **Take steps to develop vertical learning** – Practise. Practise and practise. Learn, understand, reflect, and keep transcending from one level to the next, consistently.

THE PERFECT LIBRARY DESIGN
Author's pick for this chapter

- **The Art of Learning** - Josh Waitzkin
- **The First 20 Hours: How to Learn Anything, Fast!** - Josh Kaufman
- **Design for How People Learn** - Julie Dirksen

> Visit **www.rashansenanayak.com** for the full read list and more resources.

AUDIOBOOK + PODCAST
Extended discussions available on this section, exclusively on Audible.

9

CHAPTER 9: **VALUES, MORALS & ETHICS** ⎯⎯⎯⎯⎯

I hope so far that this read is taking you through a journey of self-discovery and is laying out the tools for you to harness the potential hidden in you as you design your own definition of success.

As you move forward and get more in-depth in this process, make sure to pause, self-reflect, and identify what elements you need to tailor to your context and yourself.

(This would be a good place to pause reading, if you want more time to absorb, test, and reflect on all the tools we've already covered.)

If you are ready to move forward, let me unveil the next puzzle pieces to this life design journey: values, morals, and ethics. These essential ingredients define the core foundation on who you are and what you are capable of, not to mention your decision making process and the choices you make in life. Choices like your career pathway and how you act towards your friends, family, the planet, and everything else.

They also set you apart from everyone else and make your thinking (and, in turn, your actions) unique. Your values, morals, and ethics can – and most likely will – change and evolve over time as you learn from mistakes, interact with interesting people, and see new places. They can influence your decisions in subtle ways; sometimes they can even completely govern certain situations. The key to designing your definition of success is that you are aware of your own values, morals, and ethics and understand the strengths and weaknesses of each. If you're comfortable defending your position on any given topic in a reasonable manner with your values, morals, and ethics to back you up, you're already equipped to move on from this chapter. If you're not? Keep reading, and we'll get there together.

(If this is beginning to sound like a bunch of spiritual BS, then put those feelings aside and trust the process. Read on!)

Values

Let's step this out. First, it is important to understand exactly what constitutes a 'value'.

value
noun
the regard that something is held to deserve; the importance, worth, or usefulness of something.

Or

principles or standards of behaviour; one's judgement of what is important in life.

This is why your values deserve a lot of attention!

(So how does this relate to designing your success?)

Well, let me answer that with another question to you: "What are your own personal values?"

These are essentially values held within your own personality, and you regard them as vitally important to yourself. It is important to understand that others (family, friends, colleagues etc.) may or may not share the same values as yourself – and that's okay. Once you can clearly see this, it becomes much easier to work with people.

Let's explore and define some personal values. Authenticity, compassion, creativity, determination, fairness, fun, honesty, influence, leadership, learning, meaningful work, motivation, optimism, popularity, openness, respect, security, stability, wealth, wisdom. These are only a handful, but there are 200+ personal values that can define a person!

(This is where you need to take action!)

Download the list in the link below and highlight the ones which best align with you.

TIME TO TAKE ACTION!

Check out the downloadable resources for this section at www.rashansenanayake.com

---

Now that you have been able to gain some insights and understand what values are and how they can define you, let's take a look at why it is so important to understand your own values when designing your definition of success.

Values integrate into our core principles as a human being, as well as our Moral Compass and Spirituality.

Moral compass
noun
used in reference to a person's ability to judge what is right and wrong and act accordingly.

Therefore, to design a life that is meaningful and purposeful, our actions must be authentically aligned with our values to lead towards your own definition of success. This is what leads to a more fulfilling life and is the result of being able to derive immense happiness out of your work, your behaviour, your relationships, and ultimately lead to a life of success based on contentment – through your definition of success.

(Pin drop!)

Part of building a routine and creating sustainable habits (see chapter 22), is to practise something (almost daily) and to constantly address it in day to day decision making. For example: "Is this action I am about to take aligned with my values?"

Here's an example: My family, friends, colleagues, and acquaintances are all aware that I do not consume any alcohol/drugs. Why? Because I don't consider it fun, and enjoying myself that way is just not a value in my life. However, if I find myself in a scenario where that value is tested, how can I navigate that? – Most recently, my team and I had dinner after a conference where their meals were complimentary. Prior to the conference I considered if my company should cover their alcohol costs. Does this align with my own values at a personal level and at a business level? The answer to these questions was, simply, no. This did not mean that they were not allowed to consume alcohol – of course they can! It is a personal choice for everyone – but standing by your values means in all situations, even if there's pressure from outside. Their decision wasn't supported by my actions, but it also wasn't controlled – instead I encouraged them to make their own decision with their own resources. My team understood my reasoning and a mutual respect remains between all parties.

So, this method I am about to introduce to you can be used as a tool and integrated into your day to day life. The easiest way to use it, however, is on a year to year basis, as it allows you to reflect and allow room for change, evolution and personal growth.

(OMG! What is it?)

It is called a Values Analysis Report, where your values for that particular year are reflected, analysed, and written down with the aim of outlining what your ideal value systems are for the year ahead. This document is then reviewed, refined, and edited at the end of every year, helping you to iteratively design your ideal life.

Some call this over the top, but it works, and I have witnessed it first-hand transform my students' lives. So, what have you got to lose?

Ethics

Next up, ethics! At its core, ethics are the principles and standards that guide us in determining what is right or wrong - based on our perspective. They serve as a framework for evaluating actions and decisions in the context of their impact on others and society at large. Unlike laws, which are enforced by external authorities, ethics are largely self-regulated (though often also community-regulated), relying on your internal sense of accountability and moral reasoning.

(So, yes, you have to find your own ethical principles.)

Ethics can be seen as both personal and universal. On a personal level, ethics are shaped by your own upbringing, cultural influences, what media you consume, the people you speak to, your closest friends — the list goes on and on! This is why it is important to make sure you are careful with what you consume and who you spend most of your time with (but that is a topic for another day).

Importantly, your ethics are not static; they evolve with you, with societal changes, life experiences and new challenges, and as you develop your personality traits. For instance, modern advancements in technology and globalisation have raised complex ethical questions around privacy, environmental sustainability, social equity, and more. These shifts have highlighted the need (and importance) for each of us to critically evaluate and continuously refine their ethical stance to navigate an ever-changing world. Are we to only work towards our own individual needs and goals? Should we care about the environment? Is it important to think about the ripple effects of our career choices and the work you do?

(Can you see how critical it is to know your ethical position in life? Especially when these types of more complicated questions start to come up?)

In the context of designing your own definition of success, ethics are the gears that move you onwards (and this is not always obvious). Ethics are your guiding compass, moving you towards decisions that align with what you value while building trust, integrity, and respect in your relationships with others and with yourself. By anchoring your choices in ethical principles that resonate with you, you'll be able to pursue success in a way that not only benefits you but also contributes positively to your broader community (this is when it starts to feel as though you are doing meaningful and purposeful work. Especially in living a life that is inspired). Ethics, then, is not just about rules: it's about shaping a life of purpose and responsibility.

At its essence, your ethics are about asking fundamental questions: What should I do? and How should I live? Just like our Five Whys (Chapter 2) process from earlier, we want to get to the core of what drives us. These questions will not only guide your actions but also help you find the broader concepts that lead you towards a meaningful and responsible (and beautiful) life. Let's take a look at how we can categorise our ethics to navigate the wide-range:

- **Personal Ethics**: These are you. Your upbringing, beliefs, and experiences, and the conclusions that they inform. They influence your daily decisions and interactions regardless of magnitude.

- **Professional Ethics:** These are about your career – your contribution to society. They are standards specific to the choices you make within your careers and industries, such as honesty in journalism or confidentiality in medicine. Or simply put, this is your integrity.

- **Universal Ethics:** These are global. Principles like justice, compassion, and equality that transcend cultural and individual differences. Universal ethics connect us to the 'bigger picture' and how we choose to act within that.

As you can probably already see, these are all connected, but vary in the scale of their focus. Starting with yourself, your circle of influence, your career choices, and on to the broader principles that link us to the planet and overall humanity.

The key takeaway is that your ethics have to be about consistency – yes, consistency. Aligning our actions with our values and beliefs, authentically, rooted in good. They challenge us to act with integrity even when it's inconvenient or unpopular. So, just ask yourself:

"What legacy would you like to leave behind?"

(Take your time to answer this question to youself.You will start to see the choices and pathways ahead of you in a different light the more you focus on answering this question authentically).

Morals

On to the last piece of the puzzle: morals. Your morals are your own personal beliefs and values that guide your own sense of right and wrong. Rooted in details unique to yourself – such as cultural, religious, or familial traditions – morals are deeply ingrained in your identities and often reflect the collective norms of the society we live in. While ethics provide a broader "high-level" framework for evaluating behavior, morals are more subjective and (sometimes very) personal, influencing how we as an individual interpret and apply our ethical principles in our day-to-day life. And they're especially vital on the road towards designing our own definition of success.

At their core, morals are about what we feel we ought to do, based on what we believe is good or virtuous. They often address questions like:

- What is the right thing to do in this situation?
- How should I treat others?
- How should I allow others to treat me?
- What kind of person do I want to be?

(Some serious stuff! But, the choices we make when life forces you to answer these questions - usually circumstantially - can have ripple effects that can usually last for years, maybe even decades and in some cases, your whole life!)

For example, your current set of moral beliefs might drive you to act with honesty, generosity, or kindness, even when external pressures or circumstances make it challenging. From my own personal view, I have iterated (a fancy design word for re-designing) the above questions to fit most situations as:

- *What is the right speech?*
- *What is the right action?*
- *What is the right livelihood?*

(Side bar: Yes, these align perfectly with the <u>Buddhist philosophy of morality</u> that comprises the three stages along the '<u>Eightfold path</u>'. "If you want to know more about Buddhist morality, I'm no expert, so I'd recommend doing some Googleing to find sources who are. To help, I underlined the key phrases to search if you are interested.

Getting back on track, you can see, through my iterative process, that the word 'right' in each of the questions above is heavily linked to my own personal values and ethics, brought about through careful thought and consideration.)

–

Let's get back on track. Our morals tend to evolve over time as we ourselves do the same through encountering new experiences. They are shaped primarily by:

- **Cultural and Societal Influences**: Traditions, laws, and societal expectations often dictate what is considered morally acceptable. Essentially, what we see and do in the world around us.
- **Religious Teachings**: Some people derive their moral values from spiritual or religious doctrines that emphasise virtues such as compassion, humility, and forgiveness. You saw some of this above in my own life design.
- **Personal Reflection:** Individual experiences and critical thinking that forces or allows us to question and refine our foundational moral beliefs, particularly when we are faced with conflicting values or ethical dilemmas.

(You can see how personal this stuff can get!)

By now, you can probably notice how morals and ethics are closely related – almost two sides of the same coin – morals are far more personal and emotional, reflecting an individual's character and conscience. Ethics, on the other hand, can be seen as a more structured and universal system, sometimes bigger than us individually.

However, they will both shape the decisions we make, the relationships we build, and the life we design for ourselves (intentionally or unintentionally). Hopefully after reading this, you will be part of the 'intentional' group, setting yourself up for designing a meaningful and purposeful definition of success. And for that, we need two key elements:

1. A personal Ethical Framework
2. Our own Moral Compass

4 Steps to Designing Your Own Ethical Framework

(Here we go!)

This is the crucial part. It's one thing to learn about these concepts, but the true value, a personal definition of success, comes to those who apply the knowledge they have gained. Let's get to it.

Creating a personal ethical framework involves reflecting on your values, understanding what principles matter most to you, and deciding how to apply them consistently in your decisions and actions. This framework acts as your (ever-evolving) moral compass, helping you navigate life's complexities with clarity and integrity. What I have done here is to make it easier for you to design your own ethical framework, step-by-step, with an example story for each - all you have to do is read on and follow through with action:

1. Find Your Core Values

Start by researching and identifying the values that resonate deeply with you. These might include honesty, respect, fairness, or accountability. You already have the list downloaded from earlier in this chapter. Reflect on moments in your life when you felt proud of your actions. What values were governing you then?

Example: Maria, a young entrepreneur, realised early in her career that transparency was essential to her. After an investor offered her significant funding in exchange for compromising on product quality, Maria declined the offer. She couldn't stand the thought of lying to her customers. So while it delayed her startup's growth, she gained loyal customers who appreciated her commitment to honesty and excellence. Similarly, I follow my own values and ethical framework

in all my business decisions. This is something I always communicate to my team and I have only received nothing but support and value from the right team members.
You will find that those who do not align with your positive values will tend to conflict constantly, until it is time for you to part ways.

Write down your core values here:

_____

_____

_____

_____

(Helpful tip: Bookmark this page, or fold the corner so you can find it easier next time!)

2. Define Your Non-Negotiables

Let's get specific... What are the 'lines' you will never cross, no matter the situation? Defining these boundaries helps you stay grounded in high-pressure situations. Especially when you have the blueprint laid out, it becomes easier to navigate the tough parts of your life.

Example: Haaaaaaave you met Raj? He's a software developer working in Sydney, Australia. Raj worked on a project where his manager asked him to bypass certain privacy settings to access user data for internal marketing purposes. Despite the pressure, Raj refused, explaining that safeguarding user privacy was non-negotiable for him considering the ripple effects that his actions and work could have on people's safety. Ultimately, his decision not only protected the company's reputation but also strengthened his credibility among colleagues in the long run. You can bet that the manager also felt the consequences of these decisions, but in a very different way!

Write down your Non-Negotiables here:

_____

_____

_____

_____

3. Reflect on Ethical Dilemmas

Think about past situations where you faced difficult choices. How did you act? Was it in alignment with your core values? Could you refine those actions? Use these experiences to refine your ethical framework.

Example: Sarah is a high school teacher in Western Australia. When she caught a student cheating on a test, she faced an ethical dilemma: should she report the incident or give the student a chance to explain? Guided by her belief in fairness and compassion, Sarah chose to have an honest (yet tough) conversation with the student, uncovering personal struggles that led to them making the choice to cheat out of sheer desperation. There is always a cause and effect! The result of Sarah's choice? Together, they were able to come up with some solutions that helped the student through the tough situation and led to a better outcome for both parties. Not only that, it stopped a negative cycle, reinforcing good habits for the student.

Personally speaking, I always speak to my students to understand what is happening behind the scenes (*the cause*) to create the issue at hand (*effect*).

4. Ripple Effects!

You've already read the words 'ripple effects' a few times so far. This is because a strong ethical framework always considers not just what is right for you but also how your decisions affect others – ripple effects – or, in other words, consequences. This requires empathy (a very human skill) and the ability to see situations from multiple perspectives (a.k.a. critical thinking).

(There are plenty of documentaries these days that show the sudden awakening of individuals who never considered the ramifications (ripple effects) of their work. They never even thought about the dangers or the sheer damage that can be caused unintentionally (specially if applied in scale). The documentaries are always about the sudden realisation of these individuals and therefore deciding to take action to correct their wrongs!)

Example: David, a team leader at Costco in Southern California, USA, had to choose between laying off an employee to cut costs or finding alternative ways to reduce expenses. Driven by one of his core values, responsibility toward his team and their well-being, David found a new way to save his store's expenses by collaborating with his staff to find creative solutions. Ultimately, he avoided laying off any employees and fostered a stronger, more united team.

Consider a current choice or decision ahead of you. Reflect on the ripple effects of the choices you are currently considering and see which leads to the betterment of you, those around you, and the society at large.

That's it! Done.

Almost…

Just like most things in life, this is not set in stone! Like I've said a few times, your ethical framework should evolve as you grow and encounter new knowledge, challenges, and life experiences. Make it a habit to reflect on your values and decisions, making sure they align with the person you want to become, intentionally.

Then it's a matter of using it to guide your life. Whether it's making career decisions, or learning from challenges and successes of others, like Maria, Raj, Sarah and David, resolving conflicts, or designing your own success definition, a well-defined ethical framework helps you stay true to yourself and create a definition of success that feels fulfilling and meaningful.

Morals, Ethics, and Society

But that's easier said than done! That is because morals and ethics do not exist in isolation; they are deeply intertwined with the society in which we live. Society shapes our understanding of what is considered right and wrong, influencing personal beliefs and actions through cultural norms, laws, and collective values. At the same time, we play a crucial role in shaping and challenging societal ethics, creating a dynamic relationship that evolves over time. It's a constant tug-of-war!

(Get used to it! Get used to being uncomfortable with it.)

Challenges in Aligning Morals, Ethics, and Society

We can see this almost on a daily basis: despite their interconnectedness, conflicts often occur between our own personal morals, societal ethics, and institutional systems. These challenges can create ethical dilemmas and test one's moral integrity. Challenges like cultural and moral relativism, societal pressures and compromises, and rapidly evolving social norms and governances.

Let's take a look at some of the nuances, and a few practical strategies to help you get through.

(This is the good stuff, so take note!)

Navigating Challenges

To align morals, ethics, and societal expectations effectively, what we need to do is bolster our internal practices more with a toolkit of actions. Actions that include:

- **Personal Education:** Helps you understand diverse cultural and societal norms to build your empathy and broaden your perspectives. Knowledge is power!
- **Engage in Dialogue**: Open meaningful discussions about ethical dilemmas that lead to better solutions and mutual respect and understanding. Just make sure you're sensitive to others' needs as well as yours.
- **Stand Firm in Core Values:** While flexibility is important, knowing your own non-negotiables will help you to weather any ethical dilemmas, with clarity and purpose.
- **Become a Leader:** Societal ethics can move and evolve when individuals and groups challenge unjust systems or outdated norms. This is a sensitive area, so make sure to take action within the parameters of the law, through kindness and empathy. Remember: there is nothing in this book that talks about forcing your view on any one else.

(Just a quick note on that last point - a 'leader' is not someone that always has a label of a leader. A leader can be someone who travels to road less travelled, or someone who does the right thing, even if it is not the popular choice, or sometimes the leader is someone who sets their actions to lead by example - for whatever it might be - hopefully to do good on this planet!)

Designing Your Own Moral Compass and Ethics

Now that we have our Ethical Framework, let's work on the last piece of the puzzle – it's time to design our Moral Compass.

(Gotta love that word 'design'.)

Designing your own moral compass and ethical framework is a deeply personal journey. This usually requires new depths of honesty with yourself as you grow and evolve. It involves aligning your beliefs and values with the life you want to create. Just as you craft your definition of success, building a moral compass allows you to pursue your goals with integrity, purpose, and clarity. This process is not about aligning with a universal standard, but rather about defining what truly resonates with your authentic self while remaining considerate of the greater good.

(Inspired tip: Just like you have done before, make sure to jot down notes in the provided section to help you design as you go. Remember, they do not have to be perfect answers because this is your journey and not a social media post. So keep it private if you want, and if you are unsure, write with a pencil so you can use a pen later!)

Step 1: Clarify What Success Means to You

Start by reflecting on your vision of success. What do your professional achievements and goals look like? What about personal fulfillment? Relationships? Health? Or is it about creating positive societal impact? Defining success will provide context for the values and ethics that matter most in your journey.

Remember to be honest, guilt free! If your success definition is literally owning a ferrari, then great! But you will find as you go through life, the materialistic gains and motivations from outside yourself are usually not the sustainable success definitions in life (we talked about this in Chapter 7). Look deeper within yourself and make sure to unpack the real value you hold.

Example: Sophia, a community advocate for UNESCO, defines success as making a tangible difference in others' lives. Her moral compass is heavily rooted in compassion, equity, and collaboration. When faced with one of the most lucrative job offers of her life that conflicted with her advocacy work, she declined after careful consideration and reflection. It was more important for her to choose a path aligned with her values, even though it offered fewer financial rewards.

This was a very similar thought process I personally had when choosing to enter the business world, and it's why I ended up aligned with education.

How would you describe your definition of success?

_____

_____

_____

_____

Step 2: Identify Your Guiding Values

Following the clarification of your vision let's consider our core foundations. What are the values that form the foundation of your moral compass?

Honesty, empathy, perseverance, justice—what principles do you want to guide your actions and decisions? These values absolutely need to reflect your true aspirations and how you wish to engage with the world.

Example: Darren, a tech entrepreneur in Silicon Valley, values innovation and fairness. As his startup grew, he made a conscious decision to commit to ethical hiring practices and environmental sustainability, even when these decisions added complexity and costs and constantly turned down potential investors. For Darren, success was about leading a business that contributed positively to society, rather than materialistic quick gains.

Similarly, looking after my staff and partners well and treating their needs as my own is a consistent practice I personally follow as well and it guides almost every business decision I make.

What are the guiding values towards your success definition?

_____

_____

_____

_____

(A gentle reminder to bookmark or fold the page corner so you can come back to your own writing.)

Step 3: Anticipate and Navigate Ethical Dilemmas

Ethical dilemmas are inevitable – it's part of life! The further you progress in life, the harder the challenges are, just like in a video game. So, what's the best way to tackle this? Forecast and have your stance prepared. Your moral compass should provide clarity when you face conflicting interests or challenging choices. So make a note to ask yourself:

- Does this align with my core values?
- Who will be affected by this decision, and how?
- Will I feel proud of this choice in the future?
- What are the short term and long term ripple effects (consequences)?

Example: Tanya, a healthcare professional at a regional Queensland hospital, was faced with a tough choice between following strict hospital policy that has been placed through government hierarchy or adapting the rules to expedite care for a patient in critical need. Guided by her values of compassion and advocacy, she chose to act in the patient's best interest while transparently addressing the policy violation afterward with accountability for her actions. Naturally this was an easy decision for her since she had a clear stance on what she considered to be the right action in saving lives.

This action resulted in a reprimand from her seniors immediately. Ultimately, however, this resulted in her being seen as a leader for positive change, and she was asked to lead (with a promotion and a handsome new pay cheque) the adoption of more modern and ethical hospital policies, geared towards a more patient-centric workflow.

Step 4: Evolve & Iterate & Action it!

As you grow, your experiences and challenges will reshape your understanding of ethics and success. Be open to revisiting and refining your moral compass (personally, I tend to revisit mine yearly) to ensure it remains aligned with your evolving goals and perspectives. Not only that, your moral compass and ethical framework are only meaningful when translated into consistent action – i.e. walk the walk, don't just talk the talk. Let your principles guide how you treat others, approach challenges, and measure your achievements.

Example: Lila, a teacher at an elite private school, believes in the value of lifelong learning and empowerment. She consistently looks to design her lessons to foster curiosity and critical thinking, helping students discover their own paths to success. Her ethical commitment to education not only shapes her career but also inspires the next generation.

A practice I always follow as well, with practical application of knowledge and skills consistently shared in my classrooms in a variety of fields. The only students who miss out are the ones that do not attend!

How often would you like to refine your framework?

_____

_____

Set a date and reminder.

Back to Designing Your Definition of Success...

What we just achieved are two essential steps towards designing our own definition of success. Armed with a clearly defined moral compass and ethical framework you are set up well to take the challenges head on, resiliently. There will always be societal benchmarks like wealth, fame, or accolades that may influence societal notions of success. But, be mindful of the shiny mirror, as they often lack the depth and fulfillment that comes from living a life true to your values (connecting back to the types of motivation we have discussed in previous chapters).

By grounding your journey in a strong ethical foundation, you are set up well to ensure that your achievements are not only meaningful but also enduring. Success becomes less about external validation and more about creating a life that aligns with your authentic self, positively impacts others, and reflects the legacy you wish to leave behind.

Your moral compass is your guide through the complexities of this life – a steady force that helps you navigate challenges, make purposeful choices, and pursue a vision of success that is truly your own.

Let's keep going on this journey to design our own definition of success.

TIME TO TAKE ACTION!

**Check out the downloadable resources for this section
at www.rashansenanayake.com**

> *Our values and beliefs will always be the driving forces of our action.*

Rashan Senanayake
@rashansenanayake
www.RashanSenanayake.com

CHAPTER SUMMARY: VALUES, MORALS & ETHICS
Short summary, for a short section:

- **Value can be defined as the regard that something is held to deserve** – The importance, worth, or usefulness of something.
- **Values define who we are** – They are constantly evolving, but it is a continuous feedback loop that defines the person that we are.
- **There is an endless list of values** – Ranging from compassion to forgiveness to motivation to wealth to fame… the list goes on.
- **Understand what values are important to you** – This will shape your life and make decision making a walk in the park.
- **Develop your own ethical stance, alongside a strong moral compass** - This will help you stand tall and always find a pathway that aligns with your trueself. Even if it might not always be the popular choice.

THE PERFECT LIBRARY DESIGN
Author's pick for this chapter

- **The Road to Character** - David Brooks
- **The Moral Landscape** - Sam Harris
- **Beyond Good and Evil / On the Genealogy of Morals** - Friedrich Nietzsche
- **The Power of Ethics** - Susan Liautaud
- **How to Be Perfect** - Michael Schur

Visit **www.rashansenanayak.com** for the full read list and more resources.

AUDIOBOOK + PODCAST
Extended discussions available on this section, exclusively on Audible.

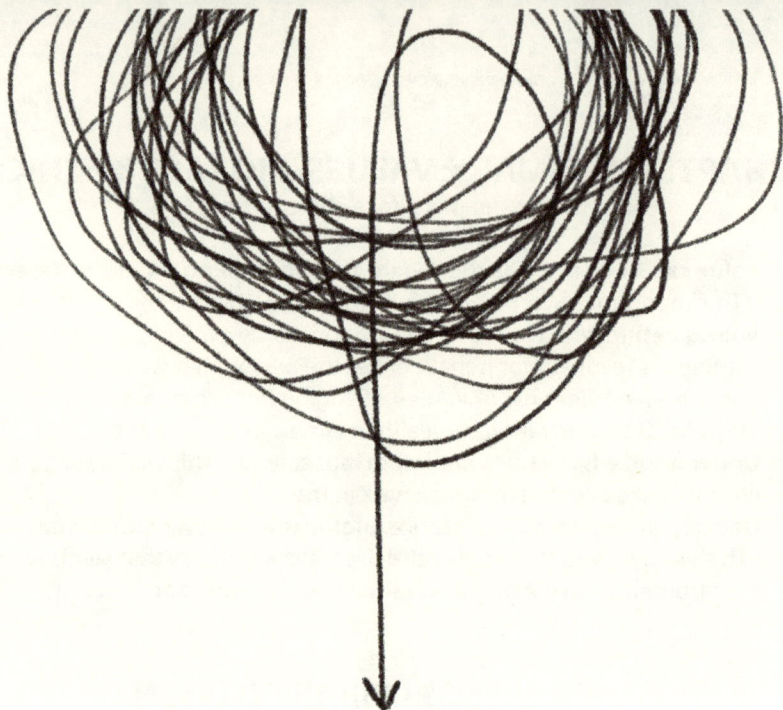

PART 3

YOUR BODY, YOUR HEALTH

DESIGNING YOUR OWN DEFINITION OF SUCCESS

PART 3: **BODY**

Moving from your mind, to your body – this vessel is the structure which we conduct all our activities through. If it fails, we fail. If it is sick, we are sick. If it is strong, we are strong (physically, in this case). Your body is a crucial element in designing your own definition of success. It allows you to physically action what needs to be done.

There are many variables that govern your physical health. Similar to your mind, your body needs regulation, fuel, healthy habits, and various other puzzle pieces to be able to function at its peak performance. The chapters in Part 3 will walk you through some variables and allow you to gain a strategic advantage in taking control of your body – by design.

*(Before we kick into gear, I want to bring on the expert knowledge into this section. Get you the right advice from the right people. I am not a PT, an exercise physiologist or even a nutritionist. So in this part of Inspired Success, you will hear my voice (or read – if you can't hear it) and that of my good friend **Daniel Jeffs** (DJ) from 'MyIdealHealth' – a Personal Trainer, Exercise Physiologist and a Physical Health Coach. He was the kid who played every sport, but just so happened to be alright at physics and chemistry too. He is the kind of guy you can train with, and then discuss stoic philosophy with over a huge steak and some wine or tequila and grapefruit juice, with, most importantly, actionable advice.*

*So, watch out for **DJ** dropping his knowledge in these chapters ahead!)*

Let's dive into the details.

10

CHAPTER 10: **BODY**

First things first! To understand your body, you need to understand the different body types. This paves the path towards being able to understand what kinds of healthy habits, nutrition, exercises, and rituals that you need to design into your life.

Body types

Ok, let's get weird! Put down the book, take your clothes off and stand in front of the mirror.

Take a good look…

What do you see?

Unless you are some sort of a genetic anomaly or a mutant, your body will fall into one of the three typical body types and shapes. The American psychologist William Sheldon in the 1940's formulated and mainstreamed these three (quite broad) categories of the human body:

- **Ectomorph**: Lean and long, with difficulty building muscle.
- **Endomorph**: Big, high body fat, often pear-shaped, with a high tendency to store body fat.
- **Mesomorph**: Muscular and well-built, with a high metabolism and responsive muscle cells.

So what does this mean? Essentially (and quite broadly), Ectomorphs tend to stay lean despite hours and hours in the gym. Endomorphs will struggle to move fat. Mesomorphs pack on muscle with ease (*Cha-ching! The genetic gold mine!*). Learning which body type you were born with (along with your blood line's various health implications) will allow you to effectively design what you need to eat and how you need to train to maximise your potential to achieve the ideal body that you want.

Knowing this, you should be aware that these body types are not the be-all and end-all. Just to make things a little bit more complicated, we are (most likely) a mix of the various types described above – usually between two body types.

So, before we move on, let's gain clarity on where you stand!

Using the world renowned Heath-Carter System, you can effectively test and identify your body type and where you stand. This is the best place to start.

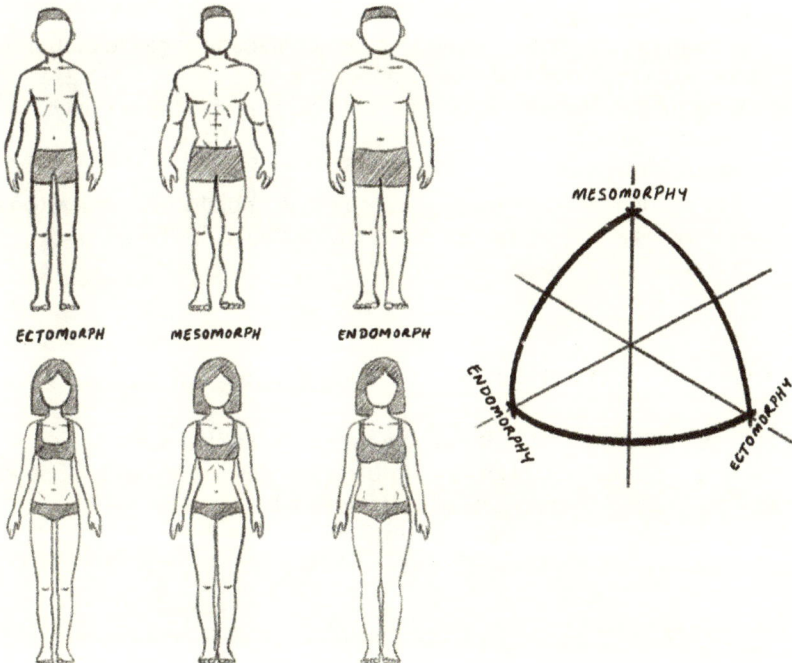

ECTOMORPH   MESOMORPH   ENDOMORPH

MESOMORPHY

ENDOMORPHY   ECTOMORPHY

Taking care of your body – or physical health – is a guaranteed gateway for unleashing your potential, making the most of every day, reaching your fullest, designing your own definition of success. A healthy body helps promote a healthy mind.

Now that you understand what type of body you have, let's take a look at the benefits and positive side-effects of designing your optimal physical health.

These are some of the positives that you can find with good physical health:

- Improved cardio-vascular health *(a healthier heart!)*.
- Manage your weight and body mass.
- Lower blood cholesterol level, reducing and sometimes preventing long term illness.
- Lower the risk of type 2 diabetes and some cancers.
- Lower blood pressure.
- Stronger bones, muscles, and joints, and a lower risk of developing osteoporosis.
- Quicker recovery from periods of hospitalisation or bed rest (or even sports/gym sessions).
- Feel better! More energy, a better mood, feel more relaxed, and sleep better.
- On top of this (and off the back of the previous chapters), there are a number of positive mental benefits that derive from good physical health.
- Through endorphin release, you can better manage negative thoughts and distract yourself from daily worries.
- Opportunity to interact with others, and do so more meaningfully.
- Improved sleep patterns.
- Improved memory.
- Change and manage levels of chemicals in your brain, such as serotonin, endorphins and stress hormones. Allowing you to feel better, think clearer and problem solve using higher brain functions.

A Quick Brain and Biochemistry Lesson!

Let's get technical and understand how each of those chemicals play a role within your physical body. How they impact your day to day life, without you even knowing that these chemical processes are happening!

Serotonin

You probably already know that serotonin plays a role in sleep and in depression, but this inhibitory chemical also plays a major role in many of your body's essential functions, including appetite, arousal, and mood. Many antidepressants target serotonin receptors to improve your mood and lessen depressive symptoms and are used to chemically alter your behaviour! This is why taking antidepressants is never a sustainable solution, unless of course you are planning on taking medication your entire life.

Dopamine

Dopamine controls many functions, including your behaviour, emotions, and cognition. This chemical also communicates with the prefrontal cortex, which is associated with pleasure and reward.

(A healthy sex life means that you are usually rich in dopamine!)

On the positive side, it helps motivate you to work toward achieving a reward. However, many illegal drugs also target dopamine receptors, contributing unnaturally to drug and alcohol addiction. Because dopamine is also related to movement, low levels of his chemical can sometimes lead to Parkinson's Disease.

Glutamate

This is the most common excitatory neurotransmitter. This usually resides throughout your brain and spinal cord. Glutamate has many essential functions, including early brain development, cognition, learning, and memory.

Norepinephrine

This chemical (a bit more complex than the others), also called noradrenaline, can sometimes act as a hormone as well. Its primary role is part of your body's stress response. It works with the hormone adrenaline to create the fight-or-flight reaction. A lot of 'stress' chemicals can eventually begin to harm your body in a negative way. So, managing this chemical plays a huge role in determining your life span as well as your physical health.

Healthy meditation practices can lead to a very positive management of norepinephrine through simple breathing techniques and managing stresses and fears.

Oxytocin

Also known as the 'cuddle' or 'love' hormone because it is usually released when people snuggle or bond socially or even play with a dog! Oxytocin is a hormone produced by the hypothalamus and secreted by the pituitary gland. This important hormone plays a crucial role in the childbirth process and also helps with male reproduction. Understanding oxytocin will help you take better care of your health and lead you toward a better understanding of how your body functions.

This can make your 'moment' more 'memorable'.

Endorphine

Endorphins are chemicals produced naturally by the nervous system to cope with pain or stress. They are often called "feel-good" chemicals because they can act as a pain reliever and happiness booster. Produced by the same areas in your brain and body as Oxytocin, this chemical is released during physical activity.

People who suffer from depression usually have much lower levels of endorphins. This is also why maintaining a healthy physical body and habits can directly link (at biophysical level) with overcoming and managing depression and anxiety.

Let's leave things there before this turns into a science textbook – and move on to food!

DJ Says:

Rashan has done what Rashan always does in this chapter, and has WAY over delivered. In this section you are going to learn about the different body types, how to utilise your time effectively by creating a workout program that actually sticks, and then enjoy the ridiculous mental health benefits that come with having a fit and strong body.

My job is to give you the most important advice of your life.

You are going to muck it all up. And that's fine.

"Thanks a lot, asshole" is what a lot of you are probably thinking right now. And you'd be right, if you didn't look deeper into what I am saying. You can write a perfect workout plan, prepare a month's worth of amazing meals and have your morning routine so dialled in that Tim Ferris himself would still muck it up.

Why?

Because you're human. And, if you're completely honest with me (and yourself), you're probably not that practised at achieving good health. Hell, when was the last time you worked out consistently for a month? A year ago? Maybe 10? Now let's add to that the stress and effort that goes into working a full time job, trying to support a family and keeping up with the ever present social schedule. The FIRST thing to go out the window is going to be your fitness plan.

But all is not lost friends, here is how you make this section of the book stick. Focus on process over product. Setting your goals around 'getting abs' or 'benching 100kg' doesn't do anything for you. It might be a good starting point, but you're only halfway there. It's the PROCESS that makes the PRODUCT, so set your goals around this. E.g. I will work on my bench 2 days per week. I will make sure my shoulder mobility routine is done every night. I will spend less than 10 hours tied to my desk today. These types of goals will actually get you somewhere.

Break your big goals into bite size chunks of process (even better if these processes are applied as weekly or daily habits) and you can achieve ANYTHING.

"

Physical fitness is the first requisite of happiness.

Joseph Pilates
Founder of Pilates

CHAPTER SUMMARY: BODY
Short summary, for a short section:

- **Understand your body type** – Design a diet and exercise regime to work towards your body type. This is the most effective method of tailoring your solutions.
- **Your brain chemistry has various elements** – Manage them or they will manage you. Design your lifestyle to make small yet positive changes to your brain chemistry.
- **Make it sustainable** – Turn healthy eating into a lifestyle as an on-going habit.

THE PERFECT LIBRARY DESIGN
Author's pick for this chapter

- **Different Bodies, Different Diets** – Carolyn Mein
- **Habits of a Happy Brain** – Loretta Graziano

Visit **www.rashansenanayak.com** for the full read list and more resources.

AUDIOBOOK + PODCAST
Extended discussions available on this section, exclusively on Audible.

11

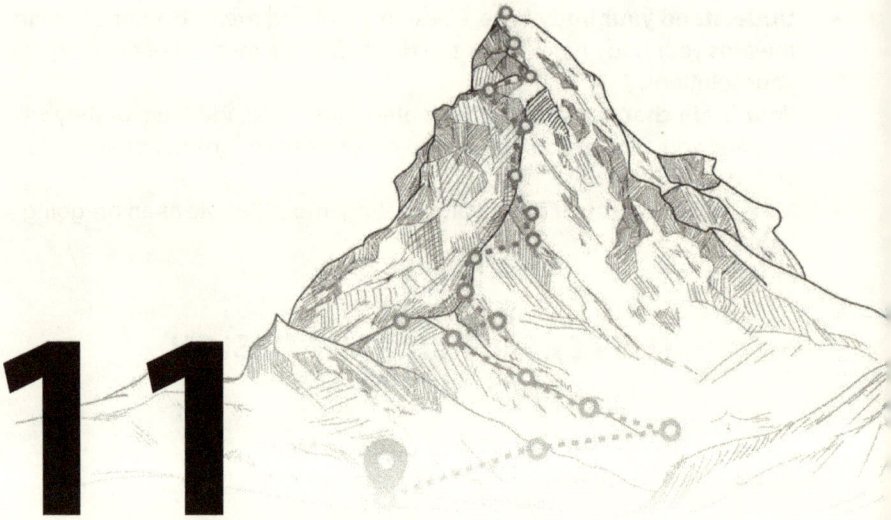

CHAPTER 11: **NUTRITION**

Fuel.

The first thing any engine requires for it to function and operate is fuel. Not just any fuel, the RIGHT fuel. If you were to put unleaded petrol into a diesel based vehicle, you would only be able to travel a mere few hundred metres before everything shuts down. Similarly, if you put jet fuel into your car, it will not mean you will be able to travel fast like a jet, simply because you have the right fuel for a jet.

You need the right fuel type that best suits your engine.
Your body is very similar.

Now that you know what your body type is, it is simply a matter of understanding what good nutritional practices best fuel your body.

Nutrition
Noun

The process of providing or obtaining the food necessary for health and growth.

"a guide to good nutrition"

This is essentially understanding how food and drink affects our bodies with a special emphasis towards the essential nutrients necessary to maintain and support your physical health. So, what does good nutrition encompass? Great nutrients (which are the various sources of energy and substance) can be classed as: carbohydrates, fats, fibre, minerals, proteins, vitamins, and water. Good nutrition means obtaining the right amount of nutrients from healthy foods in the right combinations – similar to your car fuel, but it's much more complex!

To help you design your balanced diet, I have recommended different food types for various nutrients. This is not an exhaustive list, so keep exploring – this is just the starting line!

Carbohydrates

We have a love-hate relationship with carbs. Our bodies need carbs for energy – it is as simple as that. Carbs are present in all fruits, veggies, breads and various grain products, as well as sugars. Similar to most elements, everything in moderation is the key here. Good nutrition doesn't cut out carbs, but consumes it as a controlled and balanced energy source through rich foods that are full of dietary fibres, over snacks and saturated fats/sugars/salts.

Recommended foods: oats, brown rice, sweet potato, whole wheat bread, quinoa, butternut squash

Fats

Fats don't mean getting fat! Fats are essential to our diet and are an important food group for your optimal health. There are however different fats – some being healthier and better for you than others. Try to consume unsaturated fats in a controlled manner for a balanced diet. Eating less saturated and trans fats will likely lower your risk of heart disease.

Recommended foods: omega-3 fish oils, soybean oil, nuts, yoghurts, avocados

Fibre

Fibre is one of the most crucial food groups towards our digestive health. This helps you to absorb and make the most out of your consumed foods. Fibre also helps you feel fuller for longer, as well as improve your cholesterol and blood sugar levels to assist in preventing some major diseases such as diabetes, heart disease, and bowel cancer. For an average adult over 18 years old, you need to consume approximately 30g (for males) and 25g (for females) per day.

Recommended foods: carrots (with the skin!), kidney beans, corn, broccoli, lentils, almonds, banana

Vitamins & Minerals

These are the 'colourful gems' of health that your body needs. Vitamins are divided into two groups: fat-soluble and water-soluble. Fat-soluble vitamins are found in various foods such as eggs, milk and fish oil. These don't need to be consumed every day. Vitamins A, D, E and K are fat soluble vitamins.

Looking at water-soluble vitamins – these can be extracted from veggies, dairy products and grains. Overcooking your veggies can destroy vital nutrients that your body needs! Because these are water-based, you need to consume them regularly, as your body does not store them. If your body has more than it needs, it will literally pass it away! Vitamin C and B are both water soluble.

Again, a healthy balance is the key.

When it comes to minerals, these are found in foods like cereals, bread, meat, fish, milk, dairy, nuts, fruit (especially dried fruit), and vegetables.

We need more of some minerals than others. For example, we need more calcium, phosphorus, magnesium, sodium, potassium, and chloride than we do iron, zinc, iodine, selenium and copper.

Here is your vitamin playbook (Source: Harvard Health):

Water soluble:

- **B-1**: Ham, soymilk, watermelon, acorn squash
- **B-2**: Milk, yogurt, cheese, whole and enriched grains and cereals.
- **B-3**: Meat, poultry, fish, fortified and whole grains, mushrooms, potatoes
- **B-5**: Chicken, whole grains, broccoli, avocados, mushrooms
- **B-6**: Meat, fish, poultry, legumes, tofu and other soy products, bananas
- **B-7**: Whole grains, eggs, soybeans, fish
- **B-9**: Fortified grains and cereals, asparagus, spinach, broccoli, legumes (black-eyed peas and chickpeas), orange juice
- **B-12**: Meat, poultry, fish, milk, cheese, fortified soymilk, cereals
- **Vitamin C**: Citrus fruit, potatoes, broccoli, bell peppers, spinach, strawberries, tomatoes, brussels sprouts

Fat soluble:

- **Vitamin A**: Beef, liver, eggs, shrimp, fish, fortified milk, sweet potatoes,

carrots, pumpkins, spinach, mangoes
- **Vitamin D**: Fortified milk and cereals, fatty fish
- **Vitamin E**: Vegetables oils, leafy green vegetables, whole grains, nuts
- **Vitamin K**: Cabbage, eggs, milk, spinach, broccoli, kale

Minerals:

- **Calcium**: Yoghurt, cheese, milk, salmon, leafy green vegetables
- **Chloride**: Salt
- **Magnesium**: Spinach, broccoli, legumes, seeds, whole-wheat bread
- **Potassium**: Meat, milk, fruits, vegetables, grains, legumes
- **Sodium**: Salt, soy sauce, vegetables
- **Chromium**: Meat, poultry, fish, nuts, cheese
- **Copper**: Shellfish, nuts, seeds, whole-grain products, beans, prunes
- **Fluoride**: Fish, teas
- **Iodine**: Iodized salt, seafood
- **Iron**: Red meat, poultry, eggs, fruits, green vegetables, fortified bread
- **Manganese**: Nuts, legumes, whole grains, tea
- **Selenium**: Organ meat, seafood, walnuts
- **Zinc**: Meat, shellfish, legumes, whole grains

Proteins

We love to say that we are consuming a lot of protein! It sounds cool and looks like you know what you are doing when it comes to nutrition. Well, let's get the facts right first. Protein is a macronutrient that is essential to building muscle mass. It is commonly found in animal products, though it's also present in other sources such as nuts and legumes. Chemically, protein is composed of amino acids, which are organic compounds made of carbon, hydrogen, nitrogen, oxygen and/or sulphur. Amino acids are the building blocks of proteins, and proteins are the building blocks of muscle mass.

So, the more protein you intake, the more muscle? No. A safe level of protein consumption ranges from 0.8g of protein per kg of body weight and up to 2g of protein per kg for very active athletes – the healthy range is recommended to be between 1-1.2g of protein per kg for an average person.

Protein shakes are essentially a way of supplementing the amount required for body building, weightlifting, or other athletic purposes. This essentially helps you to consume the right amount of protein to optimise a workout or training routine.

Recommended foods: Greek yoghurt, steak, chicken, salmon, tuna, cottage cheese, peanut butter, lentils, quinoa, edamame

Water

Saving the most important to the last: hydrogen and oxygen – the life sources of our body. Our physical body is approximately 60% water! Your body uses water in almost everything – cells, organs, tissues to help regulate its temperature and maintain other bodily functions. Since we lose our body's water content through breathing, sweating, and the digestive process, it is important to rehydrate by drinking water and eating foods that contain water.

Not only this, water helps you protect your tissues, spinal cord, and joints – everything is well lubricated and functions at its optimal level when you are properly hydrated. Finally, water helps your body remove any toxins and waste products in your body – this includes alcohol! And it helps your digestive process work smoothly.

Water is constantly underrated, but it is the key to life and is crucial to designing and sculpting your ideal body.

Recommended foods: Water, water and more water

Time for action! Download the template for designing your ideal balanced diet. Now this doesn't mean you have to cut out foods that you do enjoy. It is about moderation and following it through – by design.

TIME TO TAKE ACTION!

**Check out the downloadable resources for this section
at www.rashansenanayake.com**

I am known for smashing out Nutella bottles, and ask my friends, I am no stranger to KFC! However, I have been able to maintain a good, healthy, balanced lifestyle, while enjoying my favourite (good and bad) foods.

What makes it work for me is not calorie counting or following a specific routine – it's making sure 80% of my meals every week are healthy and balanced. I.e.: carbs, proteins, vitamins, minerals and the right fats. 20% of the time, I will enjoy myself with treat foods.

(Why this practice?)

Good question! This allows me to keep a flat stomach and enjoy my sports and gym routine, while allowing my body to recover quickly, as well as maintain its BMI.

Effects of Nutritious Balanced Diet

It's all about creating and sustaining healthy habits and practices. The rewards are only yours. Good nutrition can help:

- Reduce the risk of some diseases, including heart disease, diabetes, stroke, some cancers, and osteoporosis.
- Reduce high blood pressure.
- Lower high cholesterol.
- Improve your well-being.
- Improve your ability to fight off illness.
- Improve your ability to recover from illness or injury.
- Increase your energy level.

To help you kickstart habits, these are some tips for eating well:

- Eat plenty of fruits and veggies – as your Mum told you to!
- Eat plenty of whole grains – an easy way to enjoy your yummy pastas.
- Choose low fat or fat free milk – you can gain your calcium and Vit D intake to keep your bones strong.
- Choose lean meats – the lean cuts are the best *(unless you are a vegetarian/vegan)*.
- Include other sources of protein (fish, beans, tofu).

Balanced Macronutrients

You already know that your body needs the key macronutrients for normal growth and development – these are carbs, fats, proteins in larger amounts and vitamins/minerals in small amounts combined with water.

So, the most important thing is to keep your nutrition simple and make it a sustainable habit – a lifestyle. Therefore, keeping it simple will allow you to stick to it, to gain results smarter. It's up to you to design your eating plan to suit your body type, activities, and lifestyle.

I am not a believer in counting calories or counting your macronutrients – although you can if you wish – it is too complicated for me to integrate into an everyday lifestyle. What allows me to be healthy, fit, strong, agile, and achieve what I want is by using the 80 / 20 principle, combined with the *'KISS'* (*Keep It Simple Stupid*) method.

So, before we move on – KEEP. IT. SIMPLE.

The foundational rules of thumb:

- **To lose weight** – Restrict the amount of calorie intake to less than you burn.
- **To gain weight** – Consume more calories than you burn.

Simple.

However, sticking with a diet is difficult for most people, and it's the reason why so many diets fail.

To increase your chances of success on your lifestyle diet *(by design)*, individualise your macronutrient ratio based on your preferences for your health and life.

For example, people with type-2 diabetes may find it easier to control their blood sugars on a low-carb rather than a high-carb diet. Conversely, normally healthy people may find they're less hungry on a high-fat, low-carb diet, and that it's easier to follow compared to a low-fat, high-carb diet. These are proven studies.

However, diets that emphasise a high intake of one macronutrient (like fats) and low intakes of another (like carbs) are not for everyone and should be done under professional guidance!

The acceptable macronutrient distribution ranges (AMDR) guidelines set by the Institute of Medicine of the National Academies recommend that an average person should have:

- 45–65% of their calories from carbs
- 20–35% of their calories from fats
- 10–35% of their calories from proteins

In any case, choose the diet that best fits your lifestyle and preferences – and design it!. This will of course involve iterating the design. So be prepared to test and refine.

Staying Hydrated

Water. Before we move on to the next chapter, I wanted to dedicate a section to this – the magical elixir of life. The magic potion. The liquid gold – simply because of how underrated and how much we underestimate the importance of hydration. So, let's take a look at the upsides!

- Water prevents your mouth from dehydrating

Water keeps your throat and lips moist and prevents your mouth from feeling dry. Dry mouth can cause bad breath and/or an unpleasant taste – and can even promote cavities. Not to mention a dry throat can catch on various viruses and bacteria streams.

- Better cardiovascular health

Dehydration lowers your blood volume, so your heart must work harder to pump the reduced amount of blood and get enough oxygen to your cells, which makes everyday activities like walking up your stairs – as well as other movements – very difficult.

- Keeps you cool

Your body releases heat by expanding blood vessels close to the skin's surface (this is why your face gets red during exercise), kind of like your laptop or phone. This results in more blood flow and more heat dissipated into the air. When you're dehydrated, however, it takes a higher environmental temperature to trigger blood vessels to widen, so you stay hotter.

- Stay lubricated

The water inside and outside the cells of contracting muscles provides adequate nutrients and removes waste efficiently so you perform better. Water is also important for lubricating joints.

- Look younger! *(Say whaaaaaaaaaaaaaaaaaaaaaaaaa!)*

Therefore, it is a magic potion! When a person is severely dehydrated, skin is less elastic. This is different from dry skin (usually due to an external content such as soap or dry air). But drinking lots of water is not the key – it is about consistently supplying your body with adequate water. This will allow your skin to stay firm, supple and excrete toxins as they are produced during our day to day life.

- Natural cleanser for your body

Your kidneys need water to filter waste from the blood and excrete it in urine. Keeping hydrated may also help prevent urinary tract infections and kidney stones. If you are severely dehydrated, your kidneys may stop working, causing toxins to build up in your body. *(Oh no!)*

I am sure by now you are getting the understanding of how important water is to your life. As I type this sentence, I have just taken a sip of water from the bottle of water (that is always full) on my desk.

(What are the downsides?)

Well... If we look at the other end of the spectrum, these are some of the signs that your body can give:

- Little or no urine
- Urine that is darker than usual
- Dry mouth
- Sleepiness or fatigue
- Extreme thirst
- Headache
- Confusion
- Dizziness or light-headedness
- No tears when crying *(holy s***!)*

Don't wait until you notice symptoms of dehydration to take action. Actively prevent dehydration by drinking plenty of water.

So, here are some easy tips to help you stay hydrated:

- Keep a bottle of water with you during the day. To reduce your costs, carry a reusable water bottle and fill it with tap water when you can.
- If you don't like the taste of plain water, try adding a slice of lemon or lime to your drink *(yummy!)* or better yet – add fruit into your water! Strawberry and mint is one of my personal favourites.
- Drink water before, during, and after a workout/walk/training.
- When you're feeling hungry, drink water. Thirst is often confused with hunger. True hunger will not be satisfied by drinking water. Drinking water may also contribute to a healthy weight-loss plan.
- If you have trouble remembering to drink water, drink on a schedule (making it a habit). For example, drink water when you wake up, at breakfast, lunch, and dinner, and when you go to bed. Or, drink a small glass of water at the beginning of each hour. First thing I always do when I wake up is to down a full bottle of 600ml of water. This helps my body restart and it's giving your organs a wash before even getting out of bed. You will find that you will wake up much faster as well. Following every meal, I also drink a full glass of water – makes you feel full and helps with digestion. Following this habit, warm water is better than iced water.
- Drink water when you go to a restaurant. It will keep you hydrated, and it's free!

So now, it's a matter of doing it and staying hydrated!

DJ Says:

From the outside looking in, nutrition can seem like a never ending rabbit hole. It's not. It's more like the Mariana freakin' trench. Every single person in the WORLD has an opinion on what you should and shouldn't be eating, and I'm no different. But friends, all is not lost. What I am here to do for you today is to set up some principles that you can apply to your weekly food intake that keep it simple and easy to eat right.

A few things to point out first. 'Diet' just means what you put in your face. It doesn't mean restriction, it is not a simile for starving, it just means 'what are you consuming?' You can have an incredible diet high in vitamins, minerals, quality protein, carbs and fats. Or you can have a shitty diet – high sugar, processed to death and hardly recognizable as food. You are on a diet whether you like it or not. It's up to you how you feel about your choice.

My view is very similar to the founder of Crossfit, Greg Glassman. He has coached his athletes since the beginning, that you should eat meat and vegetables, nuts and seeds, some fruit, little starch, no sugar. It's simple, you can memorise it or get it tattooed on your forearm and it gives you everything you need for a solid, balanced diet.

And a quick word on the processed piece. Yes, I know that it is super easy to pound back a protein bar in between meetings but is that really what food is about. We all do it, convenience really is king from time to time, but I would urge you to eat more 'real food'. To borrow from my other food mentor (someone certainly not afraid of a chocolate tart or two) "Food shouldn't have ingredients, food IS ingredients" (Jamie Oliver).

Now here's the bit you didn't expect. I think you should have a cheat day. I think you should try your best each week to devour a plate of tacos while sipping on some tequila. I think on occasion you absolutely should find the bottom of a Ben & Jerrys pint. Just make it worth it. What I am talking about is setting a day per week that you fully invest in your happiness. Note I didn't say "throw caution to the wind and wreck all the hard work you put in through the week". By making one meal each week so exponentially important, you are simultaneously crushing every other incidental fuck up through the week. Think you are going to eat a two dollar 7/11 hot dog on a Tuesday when you know that on Saturday you have four of your best buds coming around for some pulled pork and pale ales? I think not.

Make your cheat meals incredibly high value and they will keep you on the straight and narrow throughout the week. It's that simple.

"

It takes five minutes to consume 500 calories. It takes two hours to burn them off.

Fact
Everyone who has tried it

CHAPTER SUMMARY: NUTRITION
Short summary, for a short section:

- **Understand the various effects of the different types of nutrients** – This is the foundation to help you design your ideal, enjoyable and balanced diet for your life.
- **Choose foods that you love** – Design your balanced diet to incorporate foods you love, so it becomes enjoyable and more sustainable.
- **Stay hydrated** – Water, water and more water. 'Nuff said.
- **What do you want to achieve?** – Reverse engineer the design for your balanced diet by asking yourself what you want to achieve and then how you will show up!
- **Make it sustainable** – Turn it into a lifestyle, an ongoing habit.

THE PERFECT LIBRARY DESIGN
Author's pick for this chapter

- **Nutrition in Crisis** - Richard D. Feinman
- **Good to Go** - Christie Ashwanden
- **The Complete Book of Ketones** - Mary Newport
- **Eat to Love** - Jenna Hollenstein

Visit **www.rashansenanayak.com** for the full read list and more resources.

AUDIOBOOK + PODCAST
Extended discussions available on this section, exclusively on Audible.

12

CHAPTER 12: **INTERMITTENT FASTING**

Intermittent Fasting (IF). Seems like yet another fad, a diet, a temporary thing for Instagram influencers to latch onto. Well personally speaking, it is actually far from it. Following the introduction of IF from a colleague, I have been practising the 8:16 IF routine (eat within eight hours and fast for sixteen hours each day) for over five years now and it has been nothing but a treat! The main benefits that I have been able to derive have been:

- Save more time (less eating and meal prep times)
- Consume less calories without even trying
- Enjoy more foods that I love to eat
- Sharper mind
- More energy

There are a lot of benefits to IF as well as potential downsides (as with anything) that you must be aware of and, once again, tailor to your context, body, and life in this design process.

Let's get nerdy!

Looking at what happens at a cellular level when you are following an IF lifestyle, when your body doesn't receive any food there are a number of different effects that take place. First and foremost, your body initiates cellular repair processes and manages your hormone levels to make stored body fat more accessible for energy production. Following from here, these are some of the effects that take place:

- **Insulin level changes**: Blood levels of insulin drop significantly, which facilitates fat burning faster.
- **Human growth hormone:** The blood levels within your growth hormone can increase by as much as five times. Higher levels of this hormone essentially mean that fat burning and muscle gain can occur at the same time.
- **Cellular repair**: The body kicks into gear to initiate important cellular repair processes, such as removing waste at a cellular level.
- **Gene expression**: Several changes within your genes and molecules related to longevity and protection against a variety of diseases such as Type-2 Diabetes.

(What did all that mean?)

Essentially when you fast, your insulin levels drop, and human growth hormones increase. Your cells also initiate important cellular repair processes and change your genetics to suit.

Taking a look at its other benefits, IF can:

- Help you lose weight and mid-section fats (*OMG!*). There is no surprise to this, following an IF lifestyle means that you are generally eating fewer meals and therefore you will intake less calories. Unless of course you are compensating by binge eating during your fasting times. On top of this, IF enhances your growth hormone levels and therefore with an increased amount of norepinephrine – your body breaks down body fat for its energy production. This will also increase your metabolic rate to help your body burn even more calories, faster.

- Be sharper and enhance your brain capacity. When you fast, your body has less glucose and ketones (the energy source produced when your liver burns fat). This tells your body that there is a 'food scarcity' and allows it to naturally do what it does best – survive! The result of this is that ketones will not only keep your brain sharper, but improve your cognition by growing the connection between your neurons (faster decision making and clarity) and reduce neurodegeneration.

(You mean to say that I can get smarter by following an IF lifestyle? Well, short answer yes. But more accurately, you are fine-tuning your body to do what it does best!)

- Have more energy. Building on the previous point, your body will be creating more ketones. Which means the energy it would normally take to digest, absorb and distribute foods is now used as your 'survival' energy. Which means that you will have more energy for your day to day tasks on top of better brain function.

- Save more time. This is a happy result of simply having more time from the usual time you would take for meal prep and consumptions. This gives you an additional one to two hours every day. That is approximately 730 hours every year – which equates to almost a month of your time back! All of a sudden, here is your time to gym or start that business or spend more time with your loved ones.

(Holy sh*t!...)

(Holy sh*t indeed!)

Just so you know, some of the most famous leaders, celebrities and athletes lead Intermittent Fasting lifestyles. All you have to do is Google, but to save you some time, I have listed some famous names below who follow the various types of IF practices in their lifestyle.

Types of Intermittent Fasting Practices

There are many different types (or practices) of IF currently being supported by the health industry. Each type usually gives varied results for the different body types and movement and exercise (next chapter) of each individual. These are some of the most common IF types:

Daily Fasting or 'Time Restricted Eating'

This is a sustainable method of fasting that can be incorporated into daily life – it becomes a habit, your lifestyle. As a general rule, you restrict eating into a four to eleven hour window, while the remaining thirteen to twenty hours are fasted. Essentially, you prolong your fasting period during sleep by delaying your first meal of the day, or by stopping eating earlier in the day (or both). This type of fasting is normally done on a daily basis, but some people dip in and out of it, depending on their schedule. From here, there are many different ratios that can be adopted for your life. These are some of the most common ones below:

16:8 *(This is my preferred ratio, but I also use 18:6 as well)*

The 16:8 is one of the most popular ratios of IF that can be easily incorporated into your life. Simply, you restrict eating to an eight-hour window with two to three meals, and fast for sixteen hours.

For example, your last meal at dinner may be at 8pm (plus or minus), and you can then 'break-fast' at 12pm the following day, eat (as much or as little as you want within) eight hours, and the cycle begins again.

This is by far the most manageable and has my stamp of approval.

Famous people who practise this ratio: Hugh Jackman, Nicole Kidman, Aubrey Marcus, Terry Crews, Halle Berry

20:4

The 20:4 is a type of time restrictive eating based on a twenty hour fast, with a four hour eating window. As you can imagine this is quite tough and requires a more disciplined approach. It's also recommended to consult a doctor to understand proper implications and shouldn't be attempted by novices!

Generally, with this type of ratio, you can eat till your heart (or stomach!) is content during the four-hour feasting. Simply because by default, it is difficult to consume too many calories during such a short time frame.

Longer fasts

Longer fasts are generally not done daily, but more once a week or even once a month (more common). These types of fasts are suitable for those who find they cannot commit to a daily fast, but would like to incorporate it into their weekly, monthly or yearly schedule.

If you already practise time restricted eating, you may also include longer fasts throughout the year to enhance ketosis.

(What's 'ketosis'?)

Ketosis
Noun

A metabolic state characterised by raised levels of ketone bodies in the body tissues, which is typically pathological in conditions such as diabetes, or may be the consequence of a diet that is very low in carbohydrates.

5:2 / Fast Diet

The 5:2 refers to days within a week (not hours within a day). This fast encourages fasting for two days of the week. For any two days, calories are restricted to 500 and 600 for women and men, respectively. Calories can be spread out across multiple meals throughout the day or eaten all at once. For the remaining five days, eating is not restricted by fasting.

For example, you can eat normally throughout the week, except for Tuesday and Saturday, when you only eat 500–600 calories (two meals of 250 calories, or one meal of 500kcals) in the day.

Famous people who practise this ratio: Jennifer Lopez, Benedict Cumberbatch, Jimmy Kimmel

24-hour fast

Going back to hours, the key here is to fast for 24 hours between each meal. For example, eat at 7pm on day one and fast till 7pm the next day. Alternatively, you can choose to eat earlier (for breakfast or lunch), and fast for 24 hours straight, till the next day. The idea is that you eat a meal each day but allow your body to fast for extended periods. This type of fasting is usually done once or twice per week but can be adopted more frequently.

Tip: Make sure you are well hydrated during the fasting time periods.

Famous people who practise this ratio: Kourtney Kardashian, Tim Ferris, Tom Bilyue

36-hour fast

Getting more serious… this is an extended version of the 24 hours fast. As the name suggests, you are essentially fasting (but staying hydrated) for 36 hours straight. Once again, make sure you consult your doctor before you attempt anything this extreme.

(Wowza!)

Alternate day fasting

As the name implies, this involves fasting every other day. On fasting days, eating is restricted to one meal of 500 calories, or complete fasting (zero food – only water!). Alternate days, you can eat normally (as with all fasting types, nutritional ketosis is recommended for this time.) Long-term, this is an intense method of fasting, and is quite hard to sustain – but some pros have achieved amazing results!

Spontaneous fasting / Skipping meals

This is the easiest place to begin! It's recommended for anyone who is on the fence about intermittent fasting or feels overwhelmed by setting restrictive fasting times.

This is a gentle introduction to intermittent fasting, which is led by your lifestyle and body. It is perfect for those who don't like to feel restricted or get disheartened if they don't meet the criteria of their diet.

You simply allow yourself to skip meals if you don't feel hungry or you're too busy to eat.

Spontaneous meal skipping is an effective way to recondition the popular belief that we need to eat three meals a day. You will not starve if you skip a meal now and then!

Pick the one that works best for you! Let's get fasted.

DJ Says:

IF really is the fad to end all fads. The full stop at the end of the long and convoluted story that is 'diet' over the years. For once they have come up with a program that has no crazy rules, that doesn't have you cranking back wheatgrass shakes or eating goat's testicles for breakfast (unless you want to I guess?). And here's the kicker, IF is super freakin' easy to prepare, shortens the amount of time you need to spend eating and won't turn you into a raving lunatic counting every macro and micro nutrient.

IF to me looks like this: decent quantities of good, whole foods, in ratios that make sense in time frames that are a little different to what you are used to.

That's it.

No tricks, no magic supplements, just food. In a window.

Like Rashan, IF for me has been an absolute game changer. As a Personal Trainer and Exercise Physiologist, my days start really early. Like 4:45 first client early. This means that I am generally out of bed around 3:30, finished with my morning routine by 4:10, and sipping a long black in the car on the way to the gym by 4:15. There just isn't time to fuck around in the wee hours of the morning. To make things a little more difficult, my beautiful daughter sleeps 2 doors down from the kitchen so if you think I am going to knock up a couple of eggs and some bison mince each day you are kidding yourself.

IF allows me to look after all of my morning clients and arrive happily at (my choice of) a higher fat, high protein, super veggie packed lunch by ~ 11:00. Follow that up with an afternoon snack - think some fruit, oats, protein etc and an early dinner (again to suit the little one's timeline) and I am ready for the foam roller and off to bed.

Physiological and neurological benefits aside, it's the mental wins of IF that you are really going to find incredible. It's so black and white there is literally no room for you to fuck it up.

(continued...)

1. *The office packet of TimTams gets passed around at 10:00. "No sorry, I'm fasting until lunch."*
2. *Your co-workers order in some pizza but you have an amazingly simple red duck curry on cauliflower rice and broccolini in the fridge. "uhhh… no thanks, Dominos!"*
3. *The 'afternoon sugar cravings' that usually kick in are crushed by the awesome homemade protein ball or two. "f**k YEAH!"*

If any of this gets you excited, good. It should. It's super easy and if you need any help putting a plan together let me know.

Hint: If you need a little help getting into IF, a couple of long blacks and a 'kinda' loaded teaspoon of peanut butter around 8:00 or 9:00 is a great way to get ALMOST all of the effects of IF while easing yourself in.

Good luck!

Intermittent Fasting grants us the freedom of choice and time.

This is on top of all the other many positive health benefits.

Rashan Senanayake
@rashansenanayake
www.RashanSenanayake.com

CHAPTER SUMMARY: INTERMITTENT FASTING
Short summary, for a short section:

- **Understand what you are trying to achieve** – Choose the IF lifestyle and type that works for your context and health for a long term, sustainable solution. Chat to your doctor if you have any concerns about the impact on your own health.
- **IF can be highly beneficial to your brain cognition** – Use this to your advantage and improve your career, life, relationships and/or health.
- **You have more time now!** – IF lifestyles allow you more time – an insane amount of extra time at that! So, how will you use this?
- **Make it sustainable** – Turn it into a lifestyle, an ongoing habit.

THE PERFECT LIBRARY DESIGN
Author's pick for this chapter

- **Neurofitness** - Dr. Jandial
- **Delay, Don't Deny: Living an Intermittent Fasting Lifestyle** - Gin Stephens
- **The Complete Guide to Fasting** - Dr. Jason Fun and Jimmy Moore

Visit **www.rashansenanayak.com** for the full read list and more resources.

AUDIOBOOK + PODCAST
Extended discussions available on this section, exclusively on Audible.

13

CHAPTER 13: **MOVEMENT & EXERCISE**

Onto the next piece of the puzzle – movement. More specifically, movement and exercise, because this will allow you to create a lifestyle by design for your success roadmap in designing your definition of success.

The formula to feeling good, optimising your health, having more energy *(all that jazz!)*, boils down to this proven formula:

(Balanced diet + good nutrition + hydration + movement) x consistency = Good Physical Health

exercise
Noun

activity requiring physical effort, carried out to sustain or improve health and fitness.
"exercise improves your heart and lung power"

an activity carried out for a specific purpose.
"an exercise in public relations"

Benefits of Movement & Exercise

As you could imagine from all the social media posts that you have (or have not) seen, infomercials, every parent, PT, teacher, etc. that would be trying to hammer this down your throat – there are a lot of benefits to consistently exercising. However, at the end of the day – nothing changes unless you choose to!

movement
Noun

an act of moving.

The beautiful part is, these are all results for yourself, and yourself only. Once you begin building a healthy physical body, a lot of other elements in your success journey will fall into place. These are just some of the many benefits that you can enjoy:

1. Exercise = controlled weight

Let us start with the obvious! Exercise can help prevent excess weight gain and/or help maintain weight loss. When you engage in physical activity, you burn calories. The more intense the activity, the more calories you burn – simple.

Key to gaining this benefit is consistency. If you do not have large amounts of time to go to the gym or do long jogs or play sports – that is fine. It is better to do fifteen minutes every day, than doing nothing! Try to incorporate more movement or exercise through everyday life scenarios – take the stairs instead of the elevator.

I personally always choose to take the stairs. 1. Because it's quicker; 2. It's a chance to move/exercise; 3. You can move faster than an elevator (crowded area); 4. It is the road less travelled and therefore less traffic!

2. Fight against health conditions and diseases

This may not be a worry for you if you're in your twenties and thirties. However, have you thought about your forties, fifties and sixties? Does your family have a history of diabetes, heart disease, or high blood pressure? If the answer is yes (for the majority of you, this may be for one or all of the above diseases), then you are most likely predisposed to these diseases simply through your genetics – passed down to you like precious family heirlooms! Or perhaps you are lucky and have no genetic faults, but you are a chain smoker, or enjoy the drink *(unhealthily)*, or even might be in love with your favourite snacks *(you know the type of snack I am talking about – the type of snack that doesn't love you back)*. No matter what your current weight is, being active boosts high-density lipoprotein (HDL) cholesterol, the 'good' cholesterol, and it decreases unhealthy triglycerides.

(If you got a bit confused with that last sentence, Google the words that made your head spin!)

Essentially, if you keep your blood flowing, and raise your heart rate through consistent physical movement, you will decrease cardiovascular diseases and other help problems such as:

Physical:
- Stroke
- Metabolic syndrome
- High blood pressure
- Type 2 diabetes
- Many types of cancer
- Arthritis
- Falls

Mental:
- Depression
- Anxiety
- It can also help improve cognitive function and helps lower the risk of death from all causes.

3. From mental health to improved mood

Yep – this too! There are direct studies that have over and over again effectively proven the relationship between your mental health and exercise (more on this in Part 4). Whether it's an energy lift or to blow off steam or even just to have fun (points 6 and 7!) – physical movement and exercise is your key. Physical activity stimulates various brain chemicals that may leave you feeling happier, more relaxed, and less anxious. This is what we discussed in chapter 10.

On top of all this – you will begin to also feel better about your appearance and yourself when you exercise regularly, which can boost your confidence and improve your self-esteem. You look good, you feel good!

4. Energy boosts

Do you ever have to catch your breath walking casually with your friends? Well this should be a wakeup call for you – especially if you are in your

20s/30s/40s and have no diagnosed cardiovascular diseases. Regular physical activity can improve your muscle strength and boost your endurance. This means you will have more energy throughout the day and your body will become more used to bouncing back quickly.

Exercise delivers oxygen and nutrients to your tissues and helps your cardiovascular system work smarter. And when your heart and lung health improve, you have more energy to tackle your day-to-day.

5.   Sleep like a baby!

Regular physical activity can help you fall asleep faster, get better sleep, and deepen your sleep. Just don't exercise too close to bedtime, or you may be too energised to go to sleep. Trust me – I am talking from experience. During my mid-twenties, I used to work out between 11pm-1am, then sleep. However, this had an adverse effect on my sleeping patterns and I struggled to recover (therefore lowered my exercise frequency) as well as stunted my cognitive capabilities. Now my workouts are between 6-8pm before dinner. This has optimised my sleep schedule, helps me to recover quicker, as well as helps me sleep like a baby – every night!

6.   Light the fire in your sex life

"Not tonight babe! I'm tired!". Is this you? Regular physical movement can improve energy levels and increase your confidence about your physical appearance. Let's face it – if you feel good about seeing your naked body in the mirror, you are definitely going to feel good about letting it all hang out more regularly, in front of your partner. On top of this, you can go longer *(for the guys!)* if your cardio-vascular system is fine-tuned like a racehorse! For the girls this is the same and I am willing to bet money to say that your partner will find your body more irresistible, and begin to lust after you more and more. A healthy lifestyle means that you will look good, feel good, and ultimately feel sexy – and well, we all know where that leads.

All of these results ultimately boost your sex life and can light the fire! I am only discussing 'just the tip' in this section. There is a lot more to it than you may think. So, make Google your friend – on this one. Trust me, it's worth it. For example, regular physical activity is linked with enhanced arousal for women. And men who exercise regularly are less likely to have problems with erectile dysfunction than men who don't exercise – why? Chemicals, chemicals, and more chemicals.

7.   Fun and social

Last but not least: exercise and physical activity is *(and can be, if you do not believe me)* enjoyable. It gives your body all the right things, gives you a chance to unwind, enjoy the outdoors, or simply engage in activities *(such as a sport you love)* that make you happy – releasing all the right chemicals into your body, such as serotonin. This gives you the chance to connect and develop better relationships with family or friends in a fun social setting.

So, take a dance class, hit the hiking trails *(not for me)* or join a cricket *(or another sport!)* team. Design what you enjoy, and just do it.

Exercises for Your Body Type

I am assuming you are now in the mood to go full hard at your designed exercise routine. Especially after reading the effects it can have on your sex life! Well, before you jump into it, let me now share some more valuable insights that will help you optimise your health design.

With exercise and movement: work smart, not hard.

Essentially, you could be sweatin' it out every day in the gym and eating salad leaves for every meal, but still seeing very little results. Why? It's almost always the lack of the right knowledge.

When it comes to movement and designing your health routine, understand your body type *(we already did that above in chapter 10!)*. Building on your knowledge, let's fine tune it further!

ECTOMORPH

To refresh your memory – we already know that the Ectomorph body type is naturally very thin, has narrow hips and shoulders, very low body fat and very thin arms and legs. If you are an Ectomorph – you could be saying things that annoy your Endomorph friends like, *"No matter how much I eat, I cannot seem to gain weight." ("Ohhhh… shut up!" Says your Endomorph friend)*. So, what do you need to do if you are an Ectomorph:

- **Strength Training**

Train with heavy weights and lots of rest in between sets (2-3 minutes) as well as in between exercises (5 minutes). Only train 1-2 body parts per training day to avoid too much caloric outlay. Aim for 5-10 reps and 6-8 sets of each exercise and take plenty of rest in between workouts and never train a muscle group that is sore. And if you're feeling really sore, try out foam rolling for recovery (so much fun!).

- **Cardio**

Very minimal cardio. Moderate and low-intensity bike rides and brisk walks *(think of them more as relaxing cardio activities to reduce stress).*

MESOMORPH

The Mesomorph is kind of in-between the Ectomorph and the Endomorph – my body type, but more towards an Ectomorph. They are able to put on muscle *(relatively)* easily and genetically are the ideal body type for bodybuilding *(if you want to)*. They have very strong legs, broad shoulders, and a narrower waist. Generally, they also have very low body fat as well *(depends on your diet of course!)*.

- **Strength Training**

The more varied the training, the better the results this body type will see. Light, moderate, and heavy weight training, as well as bodyweight training – it all keeps your body guessing! Basic exercises (such as push ups, squats, lunges, deadlifts, rows, chest press, shoulder press, etc.) with heavy weights, followed by isolation exercises with light to moderate weights works like a charm.

Aim for 8-12 reps for most exercises. When it comes to leg training, you can incorporate heavy weights with around 6 reps and really light or no weights at around 25-30 reps for 3-5 sets. Your frame allows for better stability.

- **Cardio**

If you want to dedicate cardio time, three days per week of cardio for 15-30 minutes is sufficient. Mix in a combination of HIIT Training *(see next section)*, or even incorporating higher reps with lower weights to activate your cardio-vascular system will also do the job.

ENDOMORPH

The Endomorph is more 'rounded' *(this does not mean 'fat' or 'obese' – that is entirely different and can affect all body types)*. They tend to store more body fat throughout the entire body naturally, especially in the legs and arms. It's much harder for the Endomorph to put on muscle, and much easier to gain weight. However, as mentioned before, you can't sit on the couch and blame your genetics! You can be thankful for the body you have and work towards becoming more fit and healthy – it may be a bit more of an effort. But has its own upsides – such as strength!

- **Strength Training**

Total-body workouts with compound movements *(see below for more about this)* are great at burning the most calories. This can be a mix of body weight training as well as moderate weightlifting.

Avoid heavy weightlifting with low reps – this will stimulate your muscles in an unproductive way for this body type. Aim for 8-12 reps and 3-5 sets for upper body and 12-20 reps for lower body.

After reaching initial weight loss goals, it is okay to start to isolate muscles you want to shape a bit more and work on your ideal physique.

- **Cardio**

Incorporate cardio a minimum of three times per week for 20-30 minutes in your target heart rate zone. Make your cardio training easy on the knees (because of the naturally larger body frame) and lower the impact with activities such as swimming, biking, hiking, and brisk walking).

These are all of course quite general and have to be tailored to your body specifically and your lifestyle, diet, routine, circumstance, and context. However, this sets your base knowledge for your body type.

FAQs

What is the Target Heart Rate Zone?

Target heart rate is defined as the minimum number of heartbeats in a given amount of time in order to reach the level of exertion necessary for cardiovascular fitness, specific to a person's age, gender, or physical fitness.

What is a Compound Movement?

Compound exercises are exercises that work multiple muscle groups at the same time. For example, a squat is a compound exercise that works the quadriceps, glutes, and calves. You can also do compound exercises that combine two exercises into one move to target even more muscles (for example, a lunge with a bicep curl).

HIIT

There have been and always will be many fitness trends evolving alongside and holding hands with what the 'ideal' body image (discussed in Part 4) is. However, HIIT (High Intensity Interval Training) has consistently been in the top three fitness best-practices for years. So, what is HIIT – other than a cool sounding word that makes you feel like an expert in exercise physiology?

HIIT means we are essentially exercising at a maximum intensity for short bursts followed by an interval, or rest period. These rest periods can be a complete stop or even a subdued active process such as walking after *(maximum effort!)* sprints.

I chose to dedicate a section to HIIT because it is something that I personally utilise and have been for over seven years and counting. It has shown the best results and you cannot argue with the science behind its benefits. It allows me to design my own physical health – that's how effective it is!

So how do you know if you are putting in the maximum effort and hitting that maximum intensity? Well, the simplest way is to hit your maximum heart rate. You can calculate your maximum heart rate by subtracting your age from 220. For example, if you're 45 years old, subtract 45 from 220 to get a maximum heart rate of 175. This is the average maximum number of times your heart should beat per minute during exercise. As you would've guessed, the older you are, the lower your maximum heart rate number. When you are young and fit you can afford to push the boundaries and elevate your heart rate as high as possible – i.e. a 20-year-old hitting 200 beats per minute. However, if a 65-year-old (max heart rate 155), was exercising to hit 200 beats per minute, they would be in a very dangerous situation for their cardiovascular health. So HIIT should be used as a tool within your means and suitable to your context – especially your age.

The ideal heart rate for effective results when engaging in HIIT is reaching the 85%+ of your maximum heart rate. To find this number, once you have your maximum heart rate, simply multiply it by 85% – i.e. a 45-year old's maximum heart rate is 175, and therefore the target range for HIIT is 148-175.

Maximum Heart Rate = (220 – (your age)) x 85%

The best way to measure this is to track your heart rate during your training. The beauty of living in an age of technology, you can wear a FitBit or an Apple Watch or other heart rate tracking device that can give you valuable data on demand. Alternatively, if you cannot afford or otherwise can't get access to wearable tech, then use your pulse - it's FREE! To check your pulse at your wrist, place two fingers between the bone and the tendon over your radial artery, which is located on the thumb side of your wrist. When you feel your pulse, count the number of beats in 15 seconds. Multiply this number by four to calculate your beats per minute.

Now that you are equipped with the right tools and techniques, let's take a look at why HIIT is so beneficial to you.

- **It's da bomb!**

HIIT is the ideal workout for a busy schedule – whether you want to squeeze in a workout during your lunch break or to get in shape within a small period of time. Research shows you can achieve more progress with consistently training fifteen minutes of interval training three times a week than the person jogging on the treadmill for an hour. And according to a 2011 study presented at the American College of Sports Medicine Annual Meeting *(a lot more studies have also confirmed this, since then)*, just two weeks of high-intensity intervals improves your aerobic capacity as much as six to eight weeks of endurance training – this is why it's da bomb!

- **Burn more fat**

Not only do you burn more calories during a HIIT workout than steady cardio, but the effect of all that intense exertion kicks your body's repair cycle into hyperdrive *(do or die!)*. That means you burn more fat and calories in the 24 hours after a HIIT workout than you do after, say, a steady-pace run. So if you're looking to get out of a morning jog with your roommate, just tell them all about this benefit of HIIT.

- **Design a healthier ticker**

Most people aren't used to pushing into the anaerobic zone *(that lovely place where you can't breathe and you feel like your heart is trying to jump out of your chest and you are going to die)*. But in this case, extreme training produces extreme results. One 2006 study found that after eight weeks of doing HIIT workouts, subjects could bicycle twice as long as they could before the study, while maintaining the same pace. Same as your muscles – the more you work them, the stronger they get.

- **Zero budget required**

Zero, zilch, na-da! Running, biking, jumping, and rowing all work great for HIIT, because you don't need any equipment to get it done. High knees, fast feet, or anything plyometric like jumping lunges work just as well to get your heart rate up fast and reap the benefits of HIIT. In fact, some equipment like dumbbells can make HIIT less effective because you want the focus to be on pushing your heart to its max, not your biceps.

- **Weight loss without muscle loss**

Have you ever wondered why the 100m sprint athletes are always shredded with amazing muscle mass – compared to the long-distance runners? Well, this is why! While steady cardio seems to encourage muscle loss, studies show that both weight training and HIIT workouts allow dieters to preserve their hard-earned muscles while ensuring most of the weight lost comes from fat stores. Cha-ching!

- **Age backwards?**

It keeps getting better! With increased fat burning and muscle preservation, HIIT stimulates the production of your human growth hormone (HGH) by up to 450% during the first 24 hours after you finish your workout. HGH is not only responsible for increased caloric burn, but it also slows down the ageing process – one of the sneaky benefits of HIIT workouts.

- **Anywhere, anytime**

"You can do it in a boat, you can do it with a goat. You can do it here or there; you can do it anywhere!" Dr. Seuss had it right! Since the concept of HIIT training is simple, you can modify it based on the time and space constraints you have and still get all the benefits and results. These workouts prove just how adaptable HIIT cardio is – and it's perfect for the 21st Century.

- **It's seriously challenging**

Last but not least – it's not easy! This is not a workout you can do while chatting with your buddy about where you are going to for dinner later today. Keep it simple – short, sharp, and focused on what you are doing – nothing else. Let's face it, if you are doing it right, you won't be able to do anything else anyway!

Try and see…

Yoga & Pilates

A very different activity to HIIT, but when it comes to your body it's very difficult to look past yoga & pilates. Both of these practices have immense benefits and it's something that even I had put off for a very long time. Before we get into the details, let's bust some myths.

1. Yoga and pilates are not just for females
2. Yoga and pilates are not for 'hippies'
3. Doing yoga and pilates does not make you any less of a 'man'

If you still have reservations about yoga and pilates, then park them aside for now and read on with an open mind and open heart.

Pilates

Pilates is a series of about 500 exercises inspired by callisthenics, yoga, and ballet. Pilates lengthens and stretches all the major muscle groups in the body in a balanced fashion to incredibly improve your flexibility, strength, balance, and body awareness.

In the 1920s, physical trainer Joseph Pilates introduced the exercises into America as a way to help injured athletes and dancers safely return to exercise and maintain their fitness. Since then, pilates has been adapted to suit people in the general community.

Pilates can be an aerobic and non-aerobic form of exercise. It requires concentration and focus, because you move your body through precise ranges of motion. Pilates lengthens and stretches all the major muscle groups in your body in a balanced fashion. It requires concentration in finding a centre point to control your body through movement. Each exercise has a prescribed placement, rhythm, and breathing patterns.

In pilates, your muscles are never worked to exhaustion (unlike HIIT), so there is no sweating or straining, just intense concentration. The workout consists of a variety of exercise sequences that are performed in low repetitions, usually five to ten times, over a session of 45 to 90 minutes.

The pilates method is taught to suit each person, and exercises are regularly re-evaluated to ensure they are appropriate for that person. Due to the individual attention, this method can suit everybody from elite athletes to people with limited mobility, pregnant women, and people with low fitness levels.

Health benefits of Pilates

- Improved flexibility.
- Increased muscle strength and tone, particularly of your abdominal

muscles, lower back, hips, and buttocks (the 'core muscles' of your body).
- Balanced muscular strength on both sides of your body.
- Enhanced muscular control of your back and limbs.
- Improved stabilisation of your spine.
- Improved posture.
- Rehabilitation or prevention of injuries related to muscle imbalances.
- Improved physical coordination and balance.
- Relaxation of your shoulders, neck, and upper back.
- Safe rehabilitation of joint and spinal injuries.
- Prevention of musculoskeletal injuries.
- Increased lung capacity and circulation through deep breathing.
- Improved concentration.
- Increased body awareness.
- Stress management and relaxation.

Pilates caters to everyone, from beginner to advanced. You can perform exercises using your own body weight, or with the help of various pieces of equipment.

A typical pilates workout includes a number of exercises and stretches. Each exercise is performed with attention to proper breathing techniques and abdominal muscle control. To gain the maximum benefit, you should do pilates at least two or three times per week. You may notice postural improvements after just 10 to 20 sessions.

Types of Pilates

The two basic forms of pilates are:
- Mat-based pilates – this is a series of exercises performed on the floor using gravity and your own body weight to provide resistance. The main aim is to condition the deeper, supporting muscles of your body to improve posture, balance and coordination.
- Equipment-based pilates – this includes specific equipment that works against spring-loaded resistance, including the 'reformer', which is a moveable carriage that you push and pull along its tracks. Some forms of Pilates include weights (such as dumbbells) and other types of small equipment that offer resistance to the muscles.

Yoga

The word yoga means 'to join or yoke together'. It brings your body and mind together, and is built on three main elements – exercise, breathing, and meditation. Yoga is an ancient Indian philosophy that dates back thousands of years. It was designed as a path to spiritual enlightenment, but in modern times, these techniques have been modified to the mainstream western culture.

There are many different varieties of yoga, but each one essentially relies on structured poses (asanas) practised with breath awareness.

Researchers have discovered that the regular practice of yoga may produce many health benefits, including increased fitness and normalisation of blood pressure. Yoga is a known cure for stress. Over time, yoga practitioners report lower levels of stress, and increased feelings of happiness and wellbeing. This is because concentrating on the postures and the breath acts as a form of meditation as well as the more regulated blood flow through your body.

The classical techniques of yoga date back more than 5,000 years. The practise of yoga encourages effort, intelligence, accuracy, thoroughness, commitment and dedication.

Types of yoga

There are many different varieties of yoga (more so these days), each with a slightly different slant and adoption. The most popular are Hatha, Bikram, Iyengar and Vinyasa yoga.

Health benefits of yoga

The practice of yoga asanas (poses) develops strength and flexibility, while soothing your nerves and calming your mind. The asanas affect the muscles, joints and skin, and the whole body – glands, nerves, internal organs, bones, respiration and the brain. The physical building blocks of yoga are the posture and the breath.

Why is yoga so beneficial to the human body?

- Cardiovascular system (heart and arteries) – asanas are isometric, which means they rely on holding muscle tension for a short period of time. This improves cardiovascular fitness and circulation.
- Digestive system – improved blood circulation and the massaging effect of surrounding muscles speeds up a sluggish digestion.
- Musculoskeletal – joints are moved through their full range of motion, which encourages mobility and eases pressure. The gentle stretching releases muscle and joint tension and stiffness, and also increases flexibility. Maintaining many of the asanas encourages strength and endurance. Weight-bearing asanas may help prevent osteoporosis and may also help people already diagnosed with osteoporosis (if practised with care under the supervision of a qualified yoga teacher). Long-term

benefits include reduced back pain and improved posture.

* Nervous system – improved blood circulation, easing of muscle tension and the act of focusing the mind on the breath all combine to soothe the nervous system. Long-term benefits include reduced stress, anxiety and fatigue, better concentration and energy levels, and increased feelings of calm and wellbeing.

Of course, unlike anything else – before you jump into it headfirst, do your research, speak to the experts, and design a program that works for your body and your context. Ultimately what may be suitable for someone else may be your kryptonite.

General exercise for a healthy lifestyle

All in all, what has been detailed so far have been various elements of a big picture health focused lifestyle for effective movement and exercise. However, we all learned how to crawl before we stood up. Then we walked a few steps, fell, and managed to eventually walk properly. Then we began jogging, and ultimately running. So, with all these elements, there is a foundation to choose from – a starting place, a step one. Building on the knowledge you have so far, it is now the right time to learn the basic exercises that can set up a strong foundation and healthy movement practices for designing your body.

Rule 1: Stick to the basics.

Do not overdo it and over complicate your health by beginning to count macros and counting calories and eating celery sticks! The key to success here is consistency, which is easy to attain when you get the basics right.

Rule 2: Do not compare your chapter 1, to another's chapter 10.

Everyone has a different journey. Do not feel bad that your friend can do 100 push ups and you cannot even muster the strength for 20. Everything happens through practice and we all need to follow our own paths.

Rule 3: Do it consistently.

You are not going to get fit or have your ideal body or even begin to make any difference working out exceedingly well one time. Not even the second day… or the third. However, if you do it consistently for a few weeks and months – you will begin to see incredible results. A focused three months of a disciplined approach can and will change your life forever.

Follow these seven exercises to build a strong foundation for 30 days (min every two days). That's all you need. Do it for yourself, your family, your partner, your… why. You will see improvements in your muscular strength, endurance, and balance. Not to mention the self-esteem boost and confidence is priceless. Oh! And your clothes will start to fit better – win!

Foundational Full Body – Workout Plan

Warm up: 5 mins light stretching – this is important. Do not skip this!

Each exercise is performed as detailed with a 2 min break in between. Bringing it down to 1 min when things begin to become easier! The beauty of this simple workout is that you can increase and decrease reps as you see fit. If you are comfortable, then, by all means – push the limit.

- Push-ups: Complete 3 sets of 25 reps.
- Lunges: Complete 3 sets of 10 reps.
- Squats: Complete 3 sets of 20 reps.
- Burpees: Complete 3 sets of 10 reps.
- Side planks: Complete 3 sets of 10-15 reps on one side, then switch.
- Sit-ups: Complete 3 sets of 15 reps.
- Glute bridge: Complete 10-12 reps for 3 sets.

Cool down: 5 min light stretching – this is important. Do not skip!

That's it! Now go and design it and do it. But make sure to tailor it to you, your own variables and context. If you are unsure of details, consult your GP or Physio before kick off.

TIME TO TAKE ACTION!

Check out the downloadable resources for this section at www.rashansenanayake.com

---

DJ Says:

Here we are. My true domain. The place that I am most comfortable. The workout section.

Yes, we are all different. Yes, you are your own unique little snowflake that has special needs, wants, and desires.

BUT. And there is always a butt (!), especially if you happen to sit on it all day. Your health and fitness is vital to designing your perfect life and is something that can simply not be overlooked or omitted. Time and time again, you will notice the top performers in all fields spruiking their incredible fitness routines. Saunas, cold plunge, ice, weights, cardio, ALL of it has hit the mainstream these days – and for a very good reason.

If you don't take care of the body, the mind suffers.

People like to imagine that there is an invisible line right around the collar bones which separates the head and body. A perfect bisection of the self into mind and body. This is bullshit. There is no possible way to separate the two. A flabby body can mean a flabby mind, and vice versa.

Too many of us spend hours on end sharpening the axe of the mind hoping to swing it like Conan only to find you have the biceps of a kindergartener. A strong mind AND strong body is what it takes.

I don't care if you have the fastest, most amazing mind on the planet – if you are laid up on valium because your back has gone out, for the eighth time this year, how good will your decision making be then?

So here's the big questions answered.

Do you need a gym?
Short answer, no. There are a plethora of exercises we can do with just your body weight, let alone a cheap and simple set up at home. But consider these facts before you decide that home workouts are for you. At home, you are going to be pulled in many directions. There will be clothes that need washing, dishes that need stacking, and lawns that need to be cut. Distractions are aplenty at home, so beware the easily-mislead!

What is the best workout plan for me?
The one that you do. Every single week I am emailed to write a program

for someone who wants a miracle fix. These people have usually had their ass handed to them by a plan scored from some bodybuilding site that has NO place in a beginner's hands. The real goal of your exercise is to prime you for success. This means that consistency over intensity is the most important factor. You simply can't outtrain consistency.

Let's say you workout SUPER hard 3 days per week but tend to miss the third most times because you are that damn sore you can't even dry your hair properly. That works out to about 110 workouts per year (running at 2.2/ week for 50 weeks). Now let's look at someone attacking the gym at 80% of their ability but 4-6 times per week and leaving the workouts feeling energised, strong, and excited to come back to the gym. Even conservatively, at 4.5 workouts per week x 50 weeks you are going to hit 225 workouts per year.

Who is looking better on the beach at summer?

The workout program that you stick to is better than the perfect plan that you could never manage anyway.

P.S Rashan is also right about the sex drive bit... bonus!

Set up a strong foundation.
Then you can build a beautiful life.

Rashan Senanayake
@rashansenanayake
www.RashanSenanayake.com

CHAPTER SUMMARY: MOVEMENT & EXERCISE
Short summary, for a short section:

- **Understand your body type** – Workout smarter and reverse engineer your design to suit your body type. This will create the shortest path to your success and to a healthy body.
- **Create a strong why and understand the benefits** – This will set up a foundation and the right routine for you to keep yourself on track.
- **Yoga and Pilates is more than just stretching** – Incorporate yoga and pilates in your design for movement and exercise for the long-term health benefits.
- **Make it fun!** – If you are having fun, then it will be more enjoyable, rather than it feeling like a chore.
- **Make it sustainable** – Design it. Action it. Turn it into a lifestyle, an ongoing habit. Above all, ensure you select something you can stick to – consistency is key!

THE PERFECT LIBRARY DESIGN
Author's pick for this chapter

- **3 Body Types** - C.K. Miller
- **Your Body Your Yoga** - Bernie Clare
- **The 4-Hour Body** - Timothy Ferriss

Visit **www.rashansenanayak.com** for the full read list and more resources.

AUDIOBOOK + PODCAST
Extended discussions available on this section, exclusively on Audible.

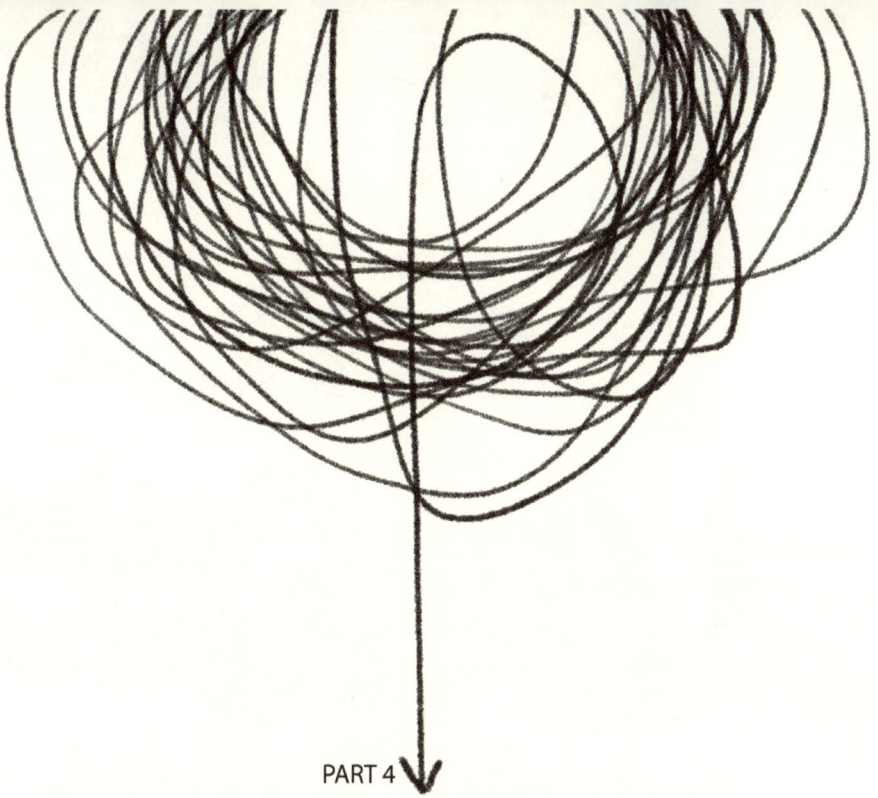

PART 4

MIND & BODY

14

PART 4: **MIND & BODY**

CHAPTER 14: **MENTAL HEALTH**

Body Image

First and foremost, these words specifically stem from Part 3: Your Body, Your Health. Which, translated, equals 'body image'. These two words have become more and more subjected to the mainstream media with magazines, TV, and social media platforms such as Instagram. Seeing others flaunt their bodies and their lifestyle practices has impacted our own perception of ourselves, our own bodies, against these 'beautiful bodies'.

So, let's discuss this delicate subject for a second.

What is Body Image?
Body image is a person's perception of their physical self and the thoughts and feelings, positive or negative or both, which results from that perception.

Positive body image occurs when a person is able to accept, appreciate, and respect their own body, in their own rights – which leads to contentment. Positive body image can make a person more resilient against the development of various mental health conditions, such as eating disorders. In fact, most of the eating disorder treatments are about undoing the bad learning habits and relearning/rebuilding self-esteem through balanced nutrition and physical activity (as discussed in the previous chapters) and possessing a positive body image about yourself.

Which means it is not your body – your perception is in your mind.

(It's in your head, man!)

However, when you know more, you can do more and be more. Breaking down the various elements of body image – there are 4 x main attributes:

- **SEE** – How you see your body in your own mind, i.e. you may consider yourself to be overweight or underweight.
- **FEEL** – How you feel about your body. This is about the satisfaction or dissatisfaction you feel about the shape or weight of your body and/or a single body part.
- **THINK** – The way you think about your own body. This is your cognitive body image, i.e. you may believe that you will feel better if you are 'skinnier' or more 'muscular'.
- **BEHAVIOUR** – How your behaviour is shaped based on the above attributes, i.e. when you are unhappy with how you look, you may socially isolate yourself and take on unhealthy and destructive habits. Alternatively, it may trigger actions to work out or eat healthier.

The behaviours are the result. It is difficult to change the resultant attribute without beginning at the grassroots level and addressing the mental aspects. How you perceive your body to be can lead to excessive exercising, eating disorders, or other negative behaviours.

On the flipside, a positive body image will improve your:

- **Self-esteem** – This will almost always dictate how you feel about your own self and stem into every aspect of your life – contributing to your happiness and wellbeing.
- **Self-acceptance** – This makes you feel comfortable and happy with the way things are, given there are so many variables, such as your genetics, habits, and nutrition. You will not be comparing your body to a Hollywood Hunk or Victoria's Secret model and feeling bad about yourself.
- **Outlook and behaviours** – This is a result and derivative of the above, as it will filter down to more balanced and healthier attitude and wellbeing practices.

From here, there is only one direction…

Mental health

One of the most debated and controversial topics that affects us all. Directly or indirectly, mental health has cast its shadow over us at one or many points in our life. It is inevitable that we must balance this important part of our wellbeing, and it is part of everyone's life journey. So, the key to designing your success definition is to firstly understand mental health and what it means for you, and then follow on to build healthy practice habits which build our resilience (discussed later).

What is mental health? According to the World Health Organisation (WHO):

Mental health
Noun

"a state of wellbeing in which every individual realises his or her own potential, can cope with the normal stresses of life, can work productively and fruitfully, and is able to make a contribution to her or his community"

It's positive! It's not a problem.

If you have not guessed already, it is very much aligned with your current journey in designing your life. Let me reiterate and break it down:

1.   *"...realising his or her own potential..."*

This is the entire premise behind Inspired Success. Designing your own definition of success and realising your own potential.

2.   *"...can cope with the normal stresses of life..."*

Through cultivated resilience, taking control of your habits (discussed later), cultivating a healthy mind and healthy body, and;

3.   *"...work productively and fruitfully..."*

To kick some major goals that align with your own why and self.

4.   *"...make a contribution to her or his community."*

Giving back. What goes around always comes around, and it's always beneficial to spend your days serving others.

Let's take a look at the flipside…

Types of mental illnesses

Before we kick on, let me be clear – I am not a mental health expert, a messiah, or a magician with gifts that are unexplainable to this world, nor is this book about curing your mental health illnesses *(if you have any)*.

My goal here is to educate and arm you with the right set of information for you to design your own definition of success. Every single thing in this book has been tried and tested, researched, and I have learned through my own Inspired Success design journey.

I decided to dedicate a section to this controversial topic simply because, through careful study, observation, and my own experiences, it is extremely evident that managing your mental health *(through the good and the bad)* is pivotal when working towards your success goals. It is even more important if you are choosing to travel along roads that are less travelled. Let me stress that mental health is a serious issue, and if you believe you are struggling in this area, there is no substitute for professional help. Stop reading right now and consult a doctor or psychologist to enable your recovery.

It's important to understand the various types of mental illnesses and look at how you might design your various habits and management strategies to each one. The key steps that have always helped me to understand, manage, and work with my mental health has been:

- **Understand the content** – which I am about to lay down in front of you.
- **Identify your own red flags** – it is a learning process to be able to identify and see the red flags of your own mental health *(which comes with practice)*. However, once identified, they can be mitigated. Prevention is better than a cure! COVID-19 has proven this to the whole world.
- **Accept and open your heart** – One of the most pivotal steps is to let yourself feel, and open your heart to accept your reality. This will help you come to terms with what needs to be done.
- **M.A.I.A, or Massive And Immediate Action!** – without procrastination. Almost as a reaction, you must get it done. If you leave this too late, then you can always reap the rewards of arriving at the finish line too late.

Personally speaking, I have refined my technique down to a few key actions which I can immediately take when red flags pop up through everyday life. If you want to learn more about my own techniques, chat to me and I will be happy to have a coffee and discuss.

Let's get to some knowledge. Understand the facts.

There are nearly 300 types of mental disorders in the DSM-5 (Diagnostic and Statistical Manual of Mental Disorders) – the handbook used by leading health professionals to help identify and diagnose various mental illnesses.

(OMG! Have you seen this book?)

(No, of course, not… I prefer to leave that to the professionals)

From these 300-odd disorders, some main groups can be categorised:

- Mood disorders (depression, bipolar disorder)
- Anxiety disorders
- Personality disorders
- Psychotic disorders
- Eating disorders
- Trauma-related disorders (such as PTSD)
- Substance abuse disorders

That's it! I am going to leave it at that. Mental illnesses can affect us all in very different ways, and I would like to respect the boundaries and allow each of you to reach out to the experts if you want to learn more and move forward. The key takeaway here is to make sure you are able to understand, accept, prevent/mitigate/sustain, and take action to manage your own mental health.

Healthy practices for your mental health

Regardless of what you may or may not have, everyone with a mind needs to protect their own mental health, even if it doesn't need immediate rescuing. There are a few key practices you can do regularly to keep your mental health in check:

- Talk about your feelings!

"OMG! What? I don't talk about feelings" – if this is you because you are a 'manly bloke' or consider yourself to be a closed off individual, talking about our feelings helps us manage a healthy mental state. It is a proven fact. So, get over it and do it. Put your trust in your family, partner, or a close friend. The trick here is to speak with one or two trusted people. Open up. Do not broadcast it to every single person you meet and try not to post about it on Facebook or on an Instagram story *(contrary to popular belief)*.

- Get active!

This was covered in the previous chapters! You already know that regular exercise can easily boost your self-esteem and your physical health will improve, allowing you to feel mentally better too.

- Eat right!

Another healthy practice covered in the previous chapters. Your body needs the right mix of nutrients to stay healthy and function in its optimal state. If your diet is good for your physical health, it is guaranteed to be beneficial towards your mental health.

- Everything in moderation

Be sensible. You eventually become what you consume. This is referring to everything from various substances *(drugs, alcohol, etc.)*, to what you hear, watch, read, etc. Everything in moderation will help you sustain a healthy mental state without permanent damage to your physical and mental health.

- Reach out, stay in touch

Drop a DM, text, or even call if you are not too cool. Reaching out to your friends and family is one of the best ways to sustain a healthy mental state and develop strong relationships.

- Ask for help

Even Superman needed the help of Batman *(the naughty brother that might be seen as dark, but deep down wants to help)*, Wonder Women *(Mother? Girlfriend? Wife?)*, Flash *(Athletic friend who is always loyal and up for a run!)* and Aquaman *(the guy who… well you get the point)* and many others. So why would you not ask for help? #askandyoushallreceive.

- Have a break, have a KitKat!

A change of scenery is just what the doctor ordered. This could be a video game, gym session, long walk, playing with your pet, or even just binge-watching Netflix (refer to the in-moderation section.). Give yourself some R&R 'me-time'.

(What's R&R? Rest & Relaxation)

- Do what you are good at

Simple. Because you cannot go wrong.

- Open the door to your heart

First and foremost, this is about you. Accept yourself for who you are and open the door to your own heart, for yourself. Extend the same courtesy to your family, friends, and *(if you are brave!)* the whole world. Don't get me wrong, this does not mean you become a pushover or let people take advantage of you. This is about accepting things for what they are instead of worrying what could/would/should happen.

- Live in the present moment

If you have depression, you are living in the past. If you have anxiety, you are living in the future. A wise man once said that the best time to live in is not the past, since you cannot change it. Not the future because it is yet to be. It is right now. That is why it is called the present. This is of course a practice cultivated through various techniques such as meditation.

- Do something to make someone else's life better

Compliment someone. Mow your neighbour's lawn *(with their permission of course)*. Help a blind person cross the road. Open a door for someone. Sponsor a child. Join a humanitarian movement. Teach someone something new. Anything from a small act of kindness to a big one, they all matter and a perfect ingredient for a positive health mental state.

66

" The best time to live in is not the past since you cannot change it. Not the future because it is yet to be. It is right now. That is why it is called a 'present'. "

Anonymous

CHAPTER SUMMARY: MENTAL HEALTH
Short summary, for a short section:

- **Understand your body image and where you stand** – Use it to fuel you and develop your own health practices.
- **Mental Health is positive** – It is not designed to be negative. Disorders are negative and these can sometimes be prevented and managed.
- **Identify the red flags** – This is the key to your success. Develop routines to mitigate and manage your red flags.
- **Live in the moment** – Not the past, because you cannot change it. Not the future, since it is yet to come. Live in the moment and you will reap the benefits of a healthy state of mind.
- **Serve others** – You simply cannot go wrong. Helping others makes you feel good!
- **Practice health habits** – Do what works. They are simple and effective practices that add up to fill the bucket that is your mental health.

THE PERFECT LIBRARY DESIGN
Author's pick for this chapter

- **The Gifts of Imperfection** - Brene Brown
- **UNFU*K Yourself** - Gary John Bishop
- **The Subtle Art of Not Giving a F*ck** - Mark Manson

Visit **www.rashansenanayak.com** for the full read list and more resources.

AUDIOBOOK + PODCAST
Extended discussions available on this section, exclusively on Audible.

15

CHAPTER 15: **GRATITUDE**

This is the antidote. The cure. The magic pill for a lot of things in our lives. It is a mindset. A practice. A ritual that paves a pathway to a happy life.

gratitude
Noun

"the quality of being thankful; readiness to show appreciation for and to return kindness."

"she expressed her gratitude to the committee for their support"

Gratitude in its raw form is extremely simple. Close to the heart and easy to practise. The results from this simple act however can be complex and rewarding at the same time.

(Why is this section in "Mind & Body?)

(Well, because practising gratitude has direct effects on your mental health as well as your physical health. Let me show you more...)

Before we get down to the details, most of us express gratitude by simply saying "thank you". Although this is a good start and an easy practice, it is much more than that. It is not just an action or a group of words. It is a strong emotion and energy that can physically rewire our brain and improve almost everything else within your life.

Gratitude is the entire outlook of our life.

Just take a second to re-read that sentence.

This is why being thankful is a start, but gratitude is the super power behind a lot of our successes (and misfortunes).

Gratitude is directly linked with appreciation, and a number of positive outcomes for you:

Improved wellbeing

It's as simple as saying thank you and meaning it. Grateful people are more pleasant, open, loveable, and easily agreeable. Have you ever seen an unhappy person who is consistently grateful? No. Because they don't exist. You cannot be an asshole if you are a grateful person.

Here's the kicker... gratitude is inversely related to mental health disorders such as depression. The positive effects of gratitude and life satisfaction have a direct link with a depressed mindset. This isn't by any means to say that gratitude is the cure for depression *(absolutely not!)*. However, gratitude practice is nearly always part of the treatment and therapy for people who struggle with depression.

Furthermore, gratitude is related inversely to depression, and positively to life satisfaction (Wood, Joseph, & Maltby, 2008). This is not to say that depressed people should simply be more grateful, as depression is a very complicated condition and a daily struggle for millions of people. Instead, perhaps gratitude practices need to be a part of the therapy and treatment for people who struggle with depression.

Try it. Just give it a go. Take a moment to be grateful to yourself. Your life to date. Focus on all the positive attributes – the people in your life, the roof over your head, the food on the table, the work you can do, the country you live in. Let that sink in...

How do you feel?

Deeper relationships

It's just what the doctor ordered when it comes to human interactions and relationships. Next time someone opens a door for you – say thank you and watch the smile on their face for receiving that gratitude from you. What about your partner? Your family? Your friends? Tell them. Verbalise it. How much you value their relationship and how grateful you are for who they are. It starts here. But people who consistently practise gratitude within their relationships are more forgiving and are less narcissistic. Naturally, that'll give your relationships a boost.

(I mean who wants to be with a selfish, unappreciative narcissist?)

All you have to do is simply have a go and watch your relationships blossom with new life with a stronger connection and satisfaction.

Glass half full!

Improved and enhanced optimism is a happy accident of gratitude practice. A groundbreaking study in 2003 explored the effects of practising gratitude and found that after ten weeks, the people who focused on gratitude showed noticeably higher levels of optimism in almost all areas of their lives including their health and exercise *(mind and body, b****!)*.

When you are optimistic about your life, your work, your health, your relationships, you are more than 65% more likely to act in a positive way which supports a healthy and happy life.

Happy life

Well, it's only natural that a happy life follows suit. Your body chemistry has changed, with happy juice flowing all through it and fuelling healthy practices. Everything is going the right way! The residual effects of a small act of kindness and gratitude can last almost weeks on end – it is a scientifically-proven, long-lasting effect for a happy life.

Therefore, the more gratitude you experience and express, the happier your life will be. Make this your life energy.

More disciplined

Ever wondered what makes some people more disciplined and have more self-control than others? They know exactly when to say no and when to action, consistently. Well the secret – the magic pill – lies in their gratitude practice. Grateful people are naturally more disciplined because their actions align with a healthy life with actions geared towards the right path. Thus, they come across as being more focused and clearer in mind.

If you have a distracted mind – try being grateful. The effects are apparent within a few weeks of consistent practice. Almost like cutting out sugar from your diet!

Better mind and body

This is just insane! A research study in 2015 (by the University of California's Davis Health Centre) showed that patients with heart failure who consistently wrote in a gratitude journal showed reduced inflammation, improved sleep, and better moods; this reduced their symptoms of heart failure after only 8 weeks.

(Are you convinced yet? No? Ok I will keep going...)

The link between the mind-body connection aligns with how gratitude can have a double benefit. For example, the feeling of appreciation helps us to have healthier minds, and with that comes healthy practices towards a healthy life and therefore a healthier body. It's like a non-stop happy, positive circle.

Gratitude = healthy mind = happy mind = healthy practices = healthy body = happy & health life

> ... adults who feel grateful have more energy, more optimism, more social connections and more happiness than those who do not, according to studies conducted over the past decade. They're also less likely to be depressed, envious, greedy or alcoholics.

Melinda Beck
Wall Street Journal Article – "Thank you, No, Thank you!"

(It keeps getting better by the way…)

Stronger neurologically-based morality

More recently, neuroscience is beginning to explore what gratitude does to the mysterious human brain, and has found signs of links to our morality, aligned with gratitude.

One study measured the brain's response to feelings of gratitude and found that gratitude increased activity in areas of the brain that deal with morality, reward, and judgement. *(O. M. G.)*

I am not an expert in human morality or neuroscience – however, simply said, it makes sense that a happy person with more focused discipline and a clear outlook will naturally have a stronger morality.

Stress reduction

Practising gratitude is a very easy way to manage the various stresses of our lives as well. I will be discussing the different types of stresses in Chapter 17 later on – but to give you a preview of what's to come – stress is a manifestation of energy in our body, in response to a given situation. So, if you are grateful for your life, the people around you, what you have etc, there is a direct link to your increased stress management ability at a chemical level.

Anyway, more on this later…

Breakdown of gratitude

At its simplest form, gratitude has two stages:

- **Internal**: The acknowledgement of the good stuff in your own life and self. Genuinely seeing your life as good and the elements within that – the material possessions, practices, your wellbeing, the relationships, future aspirations – give it texture and flavour. This is the first step: gratitude about yourself.
- **External**: Witnessing that there is a lot of good external to yourself – genuinely believing that and being able to outwardly project that to others – to people, to animals, to the world, to your material possessions. This is where the beauty lies and you can begin to see the goodness in everything. The actions from your partner never go unnoticed, the car you are driving makes you proud, the food on the table begins to nourish you more… the benefits are endless.

This will give you a full picture of the cause and effect of everything within your life through a beautiful lens and understand what makes your life just that much better!

TIME TO TAKE ACTION!

**Check out the downloadable resources for this section
at www.rashansenanayake.com**

Gratitude shapes the entire outlook of our life. It is a powerful design tool.

Rashan Senanayake
@rashansenanayake
www.RashanSenanayake.com

CHAPTER SUMMARY: GRATITUDE
Short summary, for a short section:

- **Use it to manage your stresses** – Practising gratitude is as simple as being grateful for the things already in your life. This contentment can drive your energy to achieve more from your life.
- **Use it within your relationships** – It's the secret ingredient for making all your relationships just that much better.
- **Make it a habit** – Gratitude is a practised mindset. The reward will be a better, happier, more focused self. You cannot lose.

THE PERFECT LIBRARY DESIGN
Author's pick for this chapter

- **Words of Gratitude for Mind, Body, and Soul** - Robert Emmons and Joanna Hill
- **The Gratitude Diaries** - Janice Kaplan

Visit **www.rashansenanayak.com** for the full read list and more resources.

AUDIOBOOK + PODCAST
Extended discussions available on this section, exclusively on Audible.

16

CHAPTER 16: **LETTING GO**

The snow glows white on the mountain tonight…
…

Let it go, let it go
Can't hold it back anymore
Let it go, let it go
Turn away and slam the door
I don't care what they're going to say
Let the storm rage on
The cold never bothered me anyway

Let it go, let it go
Can't hold it back anymore
Let it go, let it go
Turn away and slam the door

Let it go (go, go, go go, go go, go go, go, go, go go)
Let it go
Let it go
Let it go…

Elsa got it right!

This catchy song *(so catchy that you can hear it play while you are reading this right now!)*, has a powerful message. A message that is being embedded into the young people who love Disney! Elsa's suffering was caused by holding onto her troubles, and letting go of them made a significant impact for her to transform and re-design herself. So, let's take a closer look at what this means for you.

Let me ask you this question – do you think the glass of water half filled is too heavy for you to lift? Of course not… it's almost a bit of a stupid question to ask. Why would something so light be too heavy for you to lift? Well, let's try a small experiment.

Go to the kitchen and pour yourself a nice glass of thirst-quenching water.

(Don't drink it yet.)

Just for funzies, turn on your phone stopwatch and press start. Now, pick up the glass of water and extend your arm out straight in front of you (like you are reaching out to something) and hold on to that glass of water like your dear life depended on it.

Let's see how long you can hold on to it, until your arm becomes tired.

…

…

…

…

(Continue holding the glass of water.)

Is your arm tired yet?

Do you want to put the glass down? No? Ok… we can wait…

…

…

…

…

What about now? Still no huh? Ok…

…

…

…

…

How are you going now?

I think you should be starting to understand the lesson here. Your arm will eventually get so tired, one of two outcomes will come out of this. Either you will refuse to give up and the glass will fall out of your hand and shatter on the floor, or you will eventually put the glass down out of exhaustion.

Either way, something as light as a small glass of water will eventually become too heavy for us to keep holding on. The answer is to let it go. Put it down. Perhaps you can pick it up again when you need it.

A lot of things in our lives are very much the same. If we hold on and hold on, it will eventually become too heavy for us to hold and something will break! This is why it is important to let go, even if on a temporary basis.

So, what are the things we generally hold on to and that we can consciously let go of?

Something (tangible)

Physical things, material possessions – all things tangible. Your car, your favourite furniture items, your house, real estate, money etc. Anything and everything in the material world can be let go of.

Someone (people and relationships)

People and relationships are a tough one. However, speaking from many personal experiences, if the relationship is toxic, it is time to let go. Holding on will only do more damage to everyone involved and sometimes to the immediate people connected.

My personal philosophy is to treat everything with an open heart. This ultimately means that regardless of how they are to you, you can accept people for who they are without 'holding on'.

Emotions (both good & bad)

Emotions can be good and bad. We all want to feel the good emotions like happiness or excitement. So, when we have it, we try to hold on to it. But the more we try, the quicker it changes. The exact opposite happens with 'bad' emotions such as anger, sadness, resentment, etc. The more we hold on to these bad emotions, the more they will grow and consume us – eventually leading to changing your body's physiology.

The cure, the antidote to all lies with letting go. Good emotions – let it go. Enjoy it while it lasts without trying to hold on to it. Bad emotions – let it go. Accept them for what they are and set them free. –

Mindsets

Your mindset will determine how you approach everything – we already know this! So, let it go (by design) – i.e. if you have a fixed mindset (later discussed), learn how to let it go and adopt a growth mindset.

Habits

Another one discussed in the coming chapters. Habits are all learned. Therefore, if we can see first-hand and know factually that it is a bad habit that is moving you away from your own definition of success. Then let it go consciously and embrace positive habits.

Things beyond your control

Simple – because there is nothing you can do about it. So, let it go. If you can do something about it, then do it.

Remember! Letting go does not mean you forget. It is about releasing your grip mentally, emotionally, or even physically on what you are holding on to. Most of us hold on to something because we fear that letting go might mean that it might be forgotten. However, this is not the reality – it is about accepting it for what it is.

Letting go is a practice. It is a cultivated approach that helps you to design your own definition of success. It is important to learn:

* To UNDERSTAND WHY we should let go
* HOW to let go
* WHEN to let go
* WHAT to do when you let go

"

*If you let go a little,
you will have little peace.*

*If you let go a lot,
you will have a lot of peace.*

Ajahn Chah
Re-owned Buddhist Monk

they are – which comes in twofold.

- We let go of things beyond our control and accept the situation as it is.
- We let go in order to control what is already in our influence, accepting and putting our energy towards it. This is followed by opening your heart to the good and the bad outcomes from anything we are holding onto.

Which results in contentment and happiness. A happy life.

The pursuit of happiness is complete.

In fact, it is actually that simple!

However, the practice and application is far more difficult than the theory. Which is why, like anything else in our journey towards success, letting go needs to be cultivated through continuous practice.

How do I let go?

It comes down to the age-old question – *"How do I do it?"* Well, I am not a Buddhist monk or an expert in human psychology, however these are some of the practices that I have embedded into my life to make letting go a practice towards designing my own definition of success.

- **Use a deep breathing technique.** Just google "Square Breathing" and follow the steps.
- **Immerse yourself in a group activity.** Enjoying the people in your life may help put your problems in perspective. Talk things through, play a board game, play a sport, watch a movie, cook together – almost anything will help your mind to let go, and gain a fresh perspective.
- **Be like Bobby McFerrin.** Don't worry, be happy! Worrying may seem like it is useful, but it has no purpose. Do what you can and let go of the rest.
- **Write it down.** Write down everything on your mind that causes you to feel heavy – tasks, worries, stresses, goals. Then keep the things you want to work on and toss the rest in the bin.
- **Shift your mind.** Learn to notice when you begin thinking about something that stresses or worries you, so you can shift your thought process to something more pleasant, like something you are grateful for *(previous chapter!)*.
- **Imagine your life ten years from now.** Then look twenty years into the future, and then thirty. Will this thing matter? Most likely not…
- **Organise your space.** A clean space will reflect a clean mind. Studies have repeatedly proven that an organised space will help you clarify

thought. Not only that, completing a small task (like cleaning your desk) increases your sense of control and decreases your stress level.

- **Laugh about it.** This is about genuinely laughing out loud – so 'LOL' your way to letting go. It's proven scientifically that that laughter soothes tension, improves your immune system, and even eases pain. If you can't relax for long, start with just ten minutes watching a funny video on YouTube.

These techniques, tasks, tricks, tips, and approaches will have a different impact on every one of us in their own unique way. Use what works for you and let go of the rest.

Let go, by design.

Learning to let go is one
of the hardest lessons in life.
Letting go by design is even more difficult,
but it will shortcut your journey to your
definition of your success.

Rashan Senanayake
@rashansenanayake
www.RashanSenanayake.com

CHAPTER SUMMARY: LETTING GO
Short summary, for a short section:

- **Understand the attachment** – Understand your relationship with the various elements in your life. Know what you can and cannot let go of, and the why of doing so. Look at yourself in the third person to detach yourself for an unbiased vantage point.
- **Work out HOW, WHEN, WHAT** – To let go.
- **Clear your space** – Clear space = clear mind.
- **Practise the various habits** – Try the various methods such as deep breathing, writing, using your imagination, or even laughing out loud. Then design what works for you, and refine what doesn't.
- **Be like Elsa** – Let it go and have your heart and mind open.

THE PERFECT LIBRARY DESIGN
Author's pick for this chapter

- **The Power of Now** - Eckhart Tolle
- **The Art of Happiness** - Dalai Lama
- **You Can Heal Your Life** - Louise L. Hay

Visit **www.rashansenanayak.com** for the full read list and more resources.

AUDIOBOOK + PODCAST
Extended discussions available on this section, exclusively on Audible.

17

CHAPTER 17: **STRESS**

Letting go is something that builds on from stress, and the two have a very close relationship. It is part of our human nature to be scared of something we do not understand, so first we must understand what STRESS is, and then look at what it's all about. Let's take control of your stress.

What is stress?

Stress is a manifestation of energy in your body, as a response to a given situation. It's 100% subjective – where the same situation or context may be very stressful for you, it may not be for your colleague or family or friends. There are various types of stress, some more beneficial than others!

(Whaaaaaaaaaat?)

(Yep, you heard right…)

Stress can be a good thing! It can help you act swiftly, smartly, make you more focused, and it can help you meet deadlines or go beyond what you initially thought was possible.

On the flip side, stress can be insanely detrimental to us because it can directly affect our mental and physical health, as well as how we behave towards ourselves, our family, and our loved ones, as well as the people immediately around us. Your body can respond to stress in a variety of different ways such as producing hormones to "handle" the context (fight-or flight-mode, discussed below) – the body is naturally geared to produce chemicals to help you rise to the challenge for self-protective purposes. But, how your mindset is geared for stress can have a huge impact on these physical reactions.

Some obvious physical reactions to stress are heart rate increases, faster brain activity, and energy bursts to name a few – as I mentioned above, these are all geared into us as a natural survival instinct, going back to prehistoric times – just imagine being chased by a large sabre-tooth tiger! But too much stress can have a harmful effect on us over time. For example, if tigers were chasing you all the time… your body would be in a constant state of exhaustive stress. It is impossible for us to get rid of or avoid stress completely, but you can definitely learn how to manage it, and, better yet, harness it to your advantage.

Not all stress is bad. In fact, some stress responses can heighten your senses, helping you to avoid accidents, focus through unexpected deadlines, or to make quick decisions in chaotic situations. This is what's known as the "fight-or-flight" (or "freeze-or-fawn") response, that your body triggers in times of duress.

Quick test: Ask yourself – when someone jokingly jumps out from the dark to scare you, what is your initial reaction? Did you scream? Did you run away? Or did you step towards the person to defend yourself? Did you freeze? These are all normal responses – but it can give you a quick insight into how your mind is geared – fight or flight!

Regardless of the situation or context, stress is never truly permanent – same as everything else in this world! Your body will always return to its natural state after the stressful period has passed *(usually dictated by your mindset)*.

In our contemporary life, stress can come at us in a variety of different ways. It is no longer the fear of getting eaten by a tiger, but more about financial pressures, career commitments, deadlines, relationships, social media expectations, social status, achievements, a** hole bosses, etc. The negative side of this is that unlike in the prehistoric stress situations, our stresses can last for an extended period of time – therefore putting your body through the physical reactions to stress over a long period of time. For example: increased heart rate, constricted blood vessels, chemicals and hormones that were created for a short period of time residing in our body for much longer. Over time, these psychological stresses can cause damage to our physical health as well as lead to serious consequences like heart attacks and strokes.

Ever heard of a highly paid consultant being submitted to the hospital at the age of 35 because of a heart attack or stroke? So many times... this is often the result of too much stress. Just Google it.

Now, there is no need to be scared of *(big, bad!)* STRESS! As I mentioned above, it is a matter of being aware of it and learning how to manage and harness it to your advantage.

So let's deep-dive and take a look at the different stress types. This will help you be aware of your own stress situations and understand what to do to manage and harness them.

Types of stress

There are three main types of stress. Each one has different results, can be caused by different circumstances, and can be managed in different ways.

Acute stress

This is the most common type of stress. If you are reading this book, then you will have most likely experienced acute stress during your life. It is your body's immediate reaction to a new challenge, context, or circumstances – this is what triggers your fight-or-flight response. It is your biological response to the challenge.

What does an acute stress situation look like? A near-miss accident, an argument with a loved one, a big mistake at work, or your experience during a rollercoaster.

Acute stress is not always a bad thing because it is usually very quick and within a few hours your body will return to its natural state. Especially if you are having isolated experiences, then it will almost never have any long-term effects on your health – in fact these can be beneficial towards your health, because it gives your brain practice on how to respond to stressful situations.

Your body and mind become accustomed to handling isolated stress episodes and it increases your tolerance threshold *(especially if it is managed in a healthy way)*.

Story time! A few years ago, when I first began my journey into business, my business partner (at the time) and I were both excited and motivated about our future. Nonetheless as the months went on, the difference in opinion and various other factors began to cause undue stress to both him and I – which ultimately resulted in a mutual parting. Nonetheless, the circumstances at that time caused me (and him) a lot of acute stress. At the time it was extremely troubling, and the entire day(s) revolved around it. However, what I was unaware of at the time was that these new challenges had expanded my stress threshold and allowed my mind to learn from it. After a few years had passed, worse challenges or situations were handled in a much calmer manner, without the same response to acute stress.

This is the same with a university student stressing about first year assignments, but when they get to the final years, first year seems like a walk in the park. However, when you are in first year – it is hell on earth! This is also another example of stress thresholds expanding.

Nonetheless, severe circumstances of acute stress such as life-threatening situations can lead to long term mental health problems, including post-traumatic stress disorders or acute stress disorders.

Episodic acute stress

This is the 2.0 of acute stress, where if it begins to frequently occur in your life, episodic acute stress can occur suddenly and without warning.

Have you ever seen a person who seems to always have a crisis? Or who is short-tempered? Irritable? Anxious? Pessimistic? These are usually individuals that tend to always see the negative side of things (on an emotional level, not logical) and they tend to be more prone to episodic acute stress.

The worst part about this type of stress is that it is very difficult to change their lifestyle to improve their stress state – simply because they firmly believe or have accepted the stress as a part of their life. As a result, it will begin to have more health effects on a long-term basis and can lead to other mental states such as depression and anxiety.

This can be overcome by 'un-learning' these 'learned' behaviours to rewire your brain. There is hope after all!

Chronic stress

Here we have acute stress 3.0 – chronic stress. This is caused if acute stress isn't resolved and begins to increase as time passes. This is a constant stress and will feel as if it *"doesn't seem to go away!"*. For example, think about that metaphorical tiger who keeps chasing you every morning.

Chronic stress can be caused by major life circumstances. For example:

- Extreme financial stress (or poverty)
- A troubled or dysfunctional family
- A bad job/boss/career
- An unhappy marriage

This is the worst type of stress for your health because it is directly linked to several serious diseases and health conditions, such as heart disease, cancer, suicide, lung disease, or deliberate self-harm.

(Sheesh! That got dark real quick, didn't it?)

(Yes! Has learning about stress caused you more stress than ever before!?)

I am sharing this because ignorance is not bliss *(in this case!)*. It is important to have a clear understanding of what stress can do to you. Therefore, before we look at how to manage stresses, it is important to know what they are.

If reading this has caused you any stress – what kind of stress do you think it is?

(Seriously!?)

(Yep, I went there!)

Now that you understand what stress is and the different types, how do you manage it?

Managing stress

Stress is subjective and therefore can affect each person differently. Some people manifest it as headaches, some may get stomach aches, while others may develop insomnia or depression or get angry. Constant stress can cause you to get sick frequently, because your body chemistry isn't stable and healthy to create the right antibodies.

This is why managing stress is crucial to leading a healthy life! Even if you are Bill Gates, if you are physically unhealthy, then you cannot be your best or design your life for success.

Here are the keys to managing your stresses:

- **Acknowledge, accept, and understand** – stress cannot be removed from your life. It is part of life and must be managed, not removed. Open your heart and mind to this.
- **Search and identify what your stress causes are** – these are the things that are causing the most problems and demand the most of your energy. Ask yourself (objectively):

    What is the worst-case scenario of this situation?
    How will this change my life?
    What can I do to avoid or manage the situation?

- **Develop healthy habits such as:**
    a. **Leading a healthy life** through a healthy diet, regular exercise and a consistent sleep pattern.

    b. **Finding support**
By talking to your loved ones or friends about your problems. This helps you to get things off your chest and receive an objective opinion or support.

    c. **Being social!**
Do NOT go into a shell and isolate yourself! Even though this is what will feel easier to do. Resist the urge and find a practical way to reach out. For example, address the problem head-on by speaking to your tutor (or colleague or partner) to request help, gain an extension, build understanding and ask questions. If it gets heavy quickly, seek professional help.

    d. **Taking breaks!**
Take breaks from the things that are causing you stress. So obvious, isn't it? Yet so many people don't follow this! Think back to another stressful situation in your life – how did you manage it?

    e. **Avoid drinking or smoking your stresses away**
The bottle! A lot of people turn to it as their advisor in a stressful situation. Although it may seem to help short term (due to the loss of inhibition and temporary escape) it can actually cause more problems long term for your mental state and the problem at hand.

    f. **Reading, listening, learning, and expanding**
This means you engage and actively seek new knowledge and skill sets and grow as an individual. This will grant you a new level of self-satisfaction and sense of achievement. There are only upsides and (personally speaking) this is my favourite option.

Now, something I mentioned earlier was that stress is not always a bad thing. This is because each stress type can be managed and harnessed to have a positive or negative impact.

This is called *Eustress and Distress:*

Eustress

This is the positive type of stress. What is the result of this?

Increased motivation, focused energy, excitement, improved performance, and so much more. This is usually a short-term context and is typically brought on when the individual perceives the challenge as within their own abilities or as something they want/desire. Therefore, the stress feels like something to look forward to.

Some examples of Eustress personal stressors can be:
- An assignment deadline in a class that you enjoy
- Receiving a promotion or raise at work
- Getting married
- Buying a house/moving day
- Having a baby
- Holiday planning
- Learning about something you enjoy

Distress

The other side of the same coin is called Distress. What is the result of this?

An anxiety or worry, unpleasant or unsafe feelings, a decrease in performance, or high expectations (externally or intrinsically), can all lead to mental and physical problems (see chronic stress). This can be a short-term or long-term occurrence depending on your context, and is usually brought on when you perceive the challenge as outside of your own abilities, or as something you want or desire that cannot be reached. It becomes too overwhelming and it can feel like all hope is lost.

Some examples of Distress personal stressors can be:
- The death of a loved one
- Ending a relationship or friendship
- Conflicts in relationships
- Being abused, bullied, or neglected
- Bankruptcy and financial issues
- Unemployment

- Legal problems
- Bad life choices
- Dropping your ice cream on the floor when the tub is finished

Distress is usually derived from a variety of sources such as:
- Fears (learned fears, usually)
- Anxious thoughts (living in the future)
- Unrealistic expectations
- Perfectionist tendencies
- Procrastination
- Overcommitting

The key takeaway here is that challenges that we reactively perceive as a negative stress can be FRAMED in a positive way. When you begin to manage your stress accordingly, that's when life becomes a whole lot more easy, fun, and healthy – essential ingredients in designing your definition of success and working towards it.

> Stress comes from worrying
> about yesterday or tomorrow
> - live for today, give yourself a present.

Rashan Senanayake
@rashansenanayake
www.RashanSenanayake.com

CHAPTER SUMMARY: STRESS
Did reading through all that make you feel stressed?
Well don't worry – here is the summarised version!

- **Stress is a manifestation of energy** in your body as a response to a given situation. It's 100% subjective.
- **There are many types of stress** – Acute, chronic etc. These are essentially varying degrees of severity. Each type of stress can have a range of effects on our mental and physical health.
- **The key to managing stress is to firstly acknowledge, accept and understand** – Stress cannot be controlled or removed – it is managed.
- **Search to identify what the causes are** – Understand what is happening and see if you can take any action (within your control) to manage the situation.
- **Develop Healthy habits** – Lead a healthy lifestyle and you will have the energy to manage your stress – it's that simple!
- **Eustress can be beneficial to you** – It is usually derived from a positive challenge. It can be the source of focus, increased motivation, and willpower to achieve and strive for excellence.
- **Distress can affect your health negatively** – It can be a cause for anxiety, depression, and other mental illnesses. It is usually derived from fears, procrastination, and expectations.
- **Managing stress is all about your subjective opinion of that situation** – Reframing any situation in a positive way can help you manage and deal with your stresses.

THE PERFECT LIBRARY DESIGN
Author's pick for this chapter

- **The Upside of Stress: Why stress is good for you and how to get good at it** - Kelly McGonigal
- **Don't Sweat the Small Stuff** - Richard Carlson
- **How to Stop Worrying and Start Living** - Dale Carnegie

Visit **www.rashansenanayak.com** for the full read list and more resources.

AUDIOBOOK + PODCAST
Extended discussions available on this section, exclusively on Audible.

18

CHAPTER 18: **MINDFULNESS** —————————————

One of the most overused yet underrated words in today's society.

Let me set the scene… mindfulness was once embedded into the day-to-day culture, life, and spirituality practice of Buddhism in eastern countries (such as Sri Lanka, India, Thailand, Burma, etc.) for thousands and thousands of years.

I cannot do justice to mindfulness in this chapter as a small section of this book – it is far more complex and elaborate (yet satisfyingly simple) than what most advertising commercials and marketing brochures at your neighbourhood yoga studio suggests. Proper mindfulness takes years and years (and in the context of Buddhists – lifetimes and lifetimes) of dedication and practice.

However, what I am going to do is give you a quick understanding of what mindfulness is and how it can benefit you so that you can make conscious decisions when designing your success map and integrate it properly.

(*cough* Do it! *cough*)

What is mindfulness?

To put it simply, it is your mind's ability to be fully present. Being aware of where you are, what you are doing, understanding what the implications are and their impact on you, those around you, and the world, how you're reacting to it – your emotions, thoughts, and what is happening around you.

Easy… right?

Have you ever taken part in an activity (like an exam, assignment, task at work – something mundane) where your mind begins to wonder? You start to think about other things that you could be doing? At that moment, your mind has taken flight and is no longer present. The task at hand, what's happening around you, your body, people around, and so much more. This is because your mind is not centred on the present, but instead trying to find an alternative feeling to experience. Chasing, evolving, constantly moving.

As a result, we begin procrastinating, losing focus, and ultimately leaving room only for negative thoughts and emotions to arise from not achieving what you set out to do in the first place.

On the flipside, have you ever taken part in an activity (like playing sports, a party, playing a video game, talking to someone you love – something that you enjoy) where everything else seems to fade away and does not even enter your mind? You have no other thoughts in your mind other than that person or activity in front of you. You are present with that task or person and you are aware of your thoughts, actions, people around you. It's almost like you have heightened senses for that time period.

As a result, you are focused on one single thing and are engaged. Your body chemistry is aligned; your emotions are aligned, and you are in it presently.

The most important task… is what you are doing right now.
The most important person… is the person right in front of you.
The most important time… is right now.

For example, everyone who knows me well is aware that I am a cricket fan! I play it, I watch it, and I love it *(still not as much of a fan as my brother! But that's a story for another day)*. So, when I am playing cricket, fielding or batting or with my team – I am doing nothing but that. I am not thinking about what's going on at home, or work, or holiday planning, or chores, or any other pleasure or worries in my life. I am present in that activity and focusing on whether my body is hydrated or needs any replenishments; on what my team members are doing or saying; on studying the opposition; organising what needs to be done or speaking to the Vice-Captain about our next strategy.

Even in this activity, there are levels. I may be aware of all these things while I am on the field or off the field at the game. But when I have a cricket bat in my hands, nothing else matters other than the bowler running in and the next ball – but I am aware of my surroundings, where the fielders are standing, as well as what our score is and goal to win!

(That's all the cricket talk for now, but I must add cricket is the greatest sport of all time. If you disagree, you should come and speak to me with a good argument! The important thing to understand here is to substitute what works for you. If you can't stand cricket – then what works for you?)

So now imagine being able to be engaged and present in any activity you do, whether you like or dislike it *(that is irrelevant)*. This is the start to a mindful life. This is how you consciously architect your life's success definition.

A few things to know about mindfulness:

- **It is not something new**: It will feel familiar because it is what you already do (more or less), how you already are – it is the next level of this foundational practice.
- **It is not something extra we need to do**: You and I both have the same capacity to be 'present'. We don't need to change anything or do anything different – it is a matter of practice, and the quality of that practice. Similar to how a Personal Trainer and an obese individual working together: both have the capabilities and time to lead a healthy life, but it's just a matter of choice and circumstances.
- **You don't need to change**: It is doing what we already do, but simply *doing* what we already do, for that single task or person.
- **It is a way of life, not a fad**: It is more than just a practice. It brings awareness and care into everything we do – it cuts out unwanted stresses, baggage, and other worries and makes our lives better, one moment at a time.
- **It already works**: You have SO much proof around you (even in the modern society today) that it works. What's stopping you?
- **It gives fire to innovation:** With life becoming more and more complex, mindfulness helps you grow, keep up, develop more resilience, and help you kick goals – all without spending a single dollar!!

(Excuse my coughing earlier in this chapter - but if it helps, maybe re-read the above section and look for meaning in between the lines).

It is no surprise that the best leaders, CEOs, entrepreneurs, athletes, etc. all practice mindfulness in their own way that's designed to suit their own life and journey. All conscious decisions. All by design.

Now that you have a quick understanding of what mindfulness is (and are eager to read on), let's look at the easiest way to start and develop this practice.

How to practise mindfulness?

Western cultures have multiple labels and techniques to achieve this surface level practice. What I have practised and carried out was learned through my own personal background and upbringing.

All you have to do is breathe…

- **Step 1:** Breathe.
- **Step 2:** Keep on breathing.
- **Step 3:** Focus on breathing (especially through your nostrils).
- **Step 4:** Look at the details of breathing – how the air travels through your nose and into the lungs, your lungs expanding and contracting with each breath, how your blood flows with each breath.

Mindfulness is about moving from thinking, to feeling, to being more in tune with the present.

That's it!

Sounds easy right?

Here comes the tough part...

- **Step 5:** Do this daily and expand the time you can focus on breathing (30 secs, 1 min, 2 mins, 5 mins, 8 mins, 10 mins, 12 mins, 15 mins, 30 mins, etc.)

If you are able to develop this practice and develop the discipline to meditate, you will notice a HUGE difference in your mindset, energy, life, and a whole lot more! You will begin to handle life like a pro, kick goals and get more s*$% done, while making it look effortless!

Are you in?

(Of course you are… why wouldn't you be?)

At the risk of sounding like a meditation infomercial, here are some quick FAQs to get you started today:

- *Do I sit down?* Yes, that is the easiest way to start – but you can do walking meditation, standing meditation, and other more complex forms. But to start, definitely sit down, with your legs crossed, good posture and comfortable.
- *What if I keep thinking about other things after a short time?* That's great! It's normal… you are supposed to. Contemplate on why you are thinking like that and try to understand the cause. Come back to focus on breathing as much as you can.
- *I've tried a lot, it just doesn't work for me – when should I stop trying?* NEVER! That's why it's called a way of life! Unless you are dead, you can always try!
- *What if I don't have the time?* Then you have more reason than ever to make this a priority. You will get more out of each day when it is embedded into your way of life.

Still need more reasons – other than the fact that knowing what impact it will have on your life and the fact that the most successful individuals around the world are already doing it and the fact that it has no downside? Then go and learn more about mindfulness.

Make it a habit. Design it into your success map.

> Mindfulness is about drinking a glass of water and knowing 100% that you are drinking a glass of water.

Rashan Senanayake
@rashansenanayake
www.RashanSenanayake.com

CHAPTER SUMMARY: MINDFULNESS

It's time to bring together all your focus and be present when reading the summarised version of this chapter:

- **Mindfulness is your mind's ability to be fully present** – Being aware of where you are, what you are doing, understanding what your implications and results are and their impact on you, those around you and the world, how you're reacting to it. Your emotions, thoughts, and what is happening around you.
- **It is not something new, it is a part of nature and what we already do** – But it is about being present, and being fully aware.
- **Proper mindfulness practice is not about meditating every day** – Although it is a part of creating habits around mindfulness. It is a way of life. It is part of everything we do.
- **Mindfulness is a practice** – It's as easy as breathing, but also as difficult as not knowing you are breathing! This is the place to start.

THE PERFECT LIBRARY DESIGN
Author's pick for this chapter

- **10% Happier** - Dan Harris
- **Where You Go, There You Are** - Jon Kabat-Zinn
- **The Power of Now** - Eckhart Tolle

Visit **www.rashansenanayak.com** for the full read list and more resources.

AUDIOBOOK + PODCAST
Extended discussions available on this section, exclusively on Audible.

19

CHAPTER 19: **RESILIENCE**

"Fall down six times, get back up seven times." In fact, it should be: "Fall down six times, get back up six times"

(Think about that for a second…)

Resilience is, in fact, just that. Keep coming back, keep getting back up instead of staying down.

This one word has so much weight and impact on our lives – sometimes we don't even realise how heavy of an impact it has in our day to day life.

To me, through my own experiences, resilience is practice. Resilience is discipline. Resilience is mindset, resilience is grit, resilience is having a clear vision, resilience is clarity, resilience is **Rocky Balboa.**

Let me tell you something you already know.
The world ain't all sunshine and rainbows.
It's a very mean and nasty place and I don't care
how tough you are it will beat you to your knees
and keep you there permanently if you let it.

You, me, or nobody is gonna hit as hard as life.
But it ain't about how hard ya hit.
It's about how hard you can get hit and keep
moving forward. How much you can take and
keep moving forward. That's how winning is done!

Sylvester Stallone (as Rocky Balboa)
Actor, Director, Screenwriter, and Producer

The Story of Rocky 'Stallone' Balboa

Before we dive into understanding resilience and detailing how it can be cultivated and built, I want to take this opportunity to share the story of Rocky Balboa and how he changed my life. Prior to this however, the real reason the Rocky movies have played such a big part of my life is because I first watched Rocky IV when I was 4 or 5 years old in Sri Lanka.

(Why was a 4 year old allowed to watch an M15+ movie?! Lucky me, in Sri Lanka there were no rating systems at the time. Score…!)

It is the single most watched movie in my life, and that count will only keep growing. Easily more than five hundred times!

(Holy s**t!)

Everything, from the storyline, to the characters, to the music, to the training montages, to the final fight scenes, to how Rocky was written and made it to the big screen… It's. All. Just. Perfect!

(What do you think about the 'Creed' series, you ask? Love it! Michael B. Jordan is the perfect man for the job. The legacy.)

The Rocky soundtracks (including Creed) form the foundation of every motivational playlist that I have ever designed and used to date – everything from work motivation to gym playlists. "Eye of the Tiger", "Hearts of Fire", "Going the Distance", "No Easy Way Out", "Rocky Theme", these are all the fundamentals. Even during my university life, getting through every architecture assignment was heavily supported by the likes of Rocky.

These same practices are now carried through to my professional career and work ethic. It spills over to my sporting pursuits as well – without a doubt, every sunday morning before training, guess what I watch? Yep! That's right… Rocky! I, II, III, IV, V VI, Creed I or Creed II. It sets the tone, it sets the mindset, and it sets the focus.

(If you haven't figured it out yet – GO WATCH ROCKY! All of them...)

Personally speaking, Rocky is the epitome of resilience, mirroring Sylvester Stallone's (the actor who played Rocky) real life. At the time when Rocky was written, Stallone was completely broke, to the point where he was forced to sell his most precious possession, his dog, just so he could buy food. Not only that, he was sleeping on a park bench because he was, more or less, homeless. He used some of the last few dollars to go and watch a boxing fight as some form of entertainment and escapism from his bleak reality. Little did he know that this was the turning point of his life. He witnessed first hand during this match how the underdog triumphed over the favourite, through sheer willpower, grit, and resilience. Stallone was so inspired by this, he decided to write a screenplay for a movie and wrote the entire script for Rocky I in three straight days. He literally did nothing else other than... write!

Following this, he pitched the idea to many filmmakers and almost all rejected him, until one said that they would produce Rocky I into a movie! But under one condition – he cannot star in it. Why? Because he was not made for the big screen. Stallone, with a heavy heart, turned down the offer and kept looking, kept pitching, kept trying – rejection after rejection – until he found that one person that said yes!

(Resilience!)

But the most beautiful part about this story is that from the money he made from Rocky I *(over $100,000 in 1976!!)* the first thing he did was go find his dog and ask to buy him back! The current dog owner who bought him for only $25 *(!!!)* turned down Stallone's offer of $500, $1000, $2000, or even $5000! Because for the new owner, the dog was not for sale anymore. But that didn't stop Stallone, he kept offering more money, knowing that everyone has a price as well as knowing that nothing was going to stop him getting his dog back! Eventually an offer of $15,000 was accepted and Stallone was reunited with his beloved dog once again. *(More resilience!)*

It is the same dog that you will see in the movie Rocky I, running alongside him – best friends for life!

Rocky's character keeps moving forward despite the odds against him, defeats, failures, hardships and tough times. An unknown club level fighter going against the world heavyweight champion Apollo Creed is literally like asking a high school tech student to step into the shoes of Tim Cook (CEO of Apple Inc.). But Rocky 'goes the distance', getting up every time he is knocked down.

To go the distance.

To me (and the millions this story has inspired), this is the definition of resilience at heart.

What is Resilience?

Resilience is the ability to cope with unexpected changes and challenges in your life. It is your ability to cope with tough times by applying your inner strength and engaging support networks. Resilience can not only enable you to face difficult situations, but often provides an opportunity to further develop your coping skills. It's not always possible to prevent stressful or adverse situations, but you can strengthen your capacity to deal with these challenges.

There are many, many different ways we can show our resilience:

- Bouncing back after difficult times.
- Dealing with challenges and still holding your head up.
- Giving things a go or trying your absolute best (despite failure).
- Being strong internally.
- Being able to cope with what life throws at you and shrug it off.
- Standing up for yourself.
- Getting back into shape after you have been bent or stretched or even destroyed.
- Understanding that your mistakes are just helping accelerate your learning curve – if you allow yourself to stay resilient.

It is one of the most essential life skills that we need to practise and cultivate as a cornerstone of a growth mindset. Being able to frame and witness challenges, failures, and hardships as a learning opportunity to 'level up'!

How do you do this? Well, at its core it is quite simple. It starts with asking yourself:

- Accepting that I can't control everything: what is in my control?
- What can I do right now to get back on track?
- Can I change something I'm doing to make things better?
- What can I learn from this?
- Who can help?
- How can I move forward?

All of a sudden, reframing a challenge or a difficult situation through these questions can turn it into a learning opportunity with a positive frame of mind. It also breeds intrinsic motivation (discussed earlier) to find the energy to do things that you need to do.

This is the ultimate mental jiu-jitsu and life hack for any success journey!

Remember: "Perception is reality". There is always going to be someone else who has it better or worse than you. But your challenges and obstacles are real to you. Your resilience will make sure that you will always be okay and back to a self-actualised state in no time!

Did you just fail an exam?
Did you just drop your smartphone?
Did you get bullied?
Are you broke?
Did you lose a loved one?
Are you going through a divorce?
Did your partner cheat on you?
Did you break both your legs?
Did you find out you have cancer?

…

It doesn't matter – the key to overcoming all of it is resilience and perspective of your own situation.

How do I build resilience?

That is the right question!

Firstly, whenever a small challenge or a traumatic event in our life happens, the result that causes our distress is stress. This can lead to various mental health conditions such as anxiety and depression, or even lead to various physical conditions such as strokes or a heart attack. Or even the stress can slowly age you without you even knowing! We spoke about stress previously in this book, and a key part of building resilience is to understand how we can cope with the resultant stress, which is projected from these challenging life events.

Various stress coping strategies can enable you to deal with stress and maintain a sense of control in your life. There are many different ways of coping with your stresses and everyone is different, so it's about finding something that works for you – design it to suit your life! This is pivotal in designing your own success journey. Anything that is not harmful to your health and wellbeing could be worth a try, such as:

- Taking time out to relax
- Exercise *(the one I prefer!)*
- Meditation
- Breaking a challenge down into small, achievable goals
- Celebrating achieving your goals *(big or small)*
- Keeping a journal

- Thinking about the bigger picture
- Speaking to others
- Practising gratitude

These coping strategies give you the much needed mental and physical energy to positively reframe and cope with what is ahead (or behind) of you. From here, double-down on it by:

- Knowing your strengths and improving them,
- Stepping up and out of your comfort zone – a great way to build resilience. Attack your fears head on. Don't let them hang over your head.
- Looking after yourself – if you need to binge on a TV show to take time off, then giving yourself permission.
- Keep trying – never giving up (even if you fail) – Ask yourself, "What would Rocky do?" It works for me.
- Learn from your mistakes. Don't make them again.
- Accept that change is the only inevitable truth in this world.
- Building your self-esteem – have confidence in your abilities and the positive things in life.
- Build healthy relationships. This includes removing unhealthy ones, by design.
- Knowing when to ask for help. No one is alone! Don't let your ego dictate things. Reach out.
- Manage your stress and anxiety levels. How? Previous dot points.
- Working on problem solving skills and coping strategies – chipping away at it and taking things one day at a time.

These are not to be approached as a tick box checklist. But more as an approach to your life, your context, and your situation and challenges.

Challenges are a part of life, but remember...

"

... it ain't about how hard you can hit - it's about how hard you can get hit and keep moving forward! That's how winning is done!

Sylvester Stallone (as Rocky Balboa)
Actor, Director, Screenwriter, and Producer

(*goosebumps*)
This is the key to a strong, resilient, successful, inspired life.

Everybody comes to a point in their life when they want to quit, but it's what you do at that moment that determines who you really are.

David Goggins
World's Toughest Man

Resilience is the real,
true test of your character.

Rashan Senanayake
@rashansenanayake
www.RashanSenanayake.com

CHAPTER SUMMARY: RESILIENCE
Let's take a look at the key summaries from this chapter:

- **Resilience is the ability to cope with unexpected changes and challenges in your life** – It's what keeps us going and helps us decide to get back up that one more time.
- **Challenges will come, challenges will go** – It is about how we manage and respond to these challenges that will define who we are.
- **It is subjective** – Therefore do what works for you! Find out what works for you. You may already be naturally resilient. If so, how can you double down on this?
- **Build resilience into your life and integrate a growth mindset** – See failure, challenges, and hardship as a learning opportunity.
- **Do what is in your control** – Look after your health, your day-to-day actions and take things one day at a time, living in the present moment.
- **Perception is reality** – Don't ever compare yourself to others and learn to be kind to yourself; give yourself permission to overcome obstacles and grow.

THE PERFECT LIBRARY DESIGN
Author's pick for this chapter

- **Grit** - Angela Duckworth
- **Can't Hurt Me** - David Goggins
- **Resilience** - Eric Grietens
- **Developing Resilience: A Cognitive Behavioural Approach** - Michael Neenan
- **Extreme Ownership** - Jocko Willink & Leif Babin

Visit **www.rashansenanayak.com** for the full read list and more resources.

AUDIOBOOK + PODCAST
Extended discussions available on this section, exclusively on Audible.

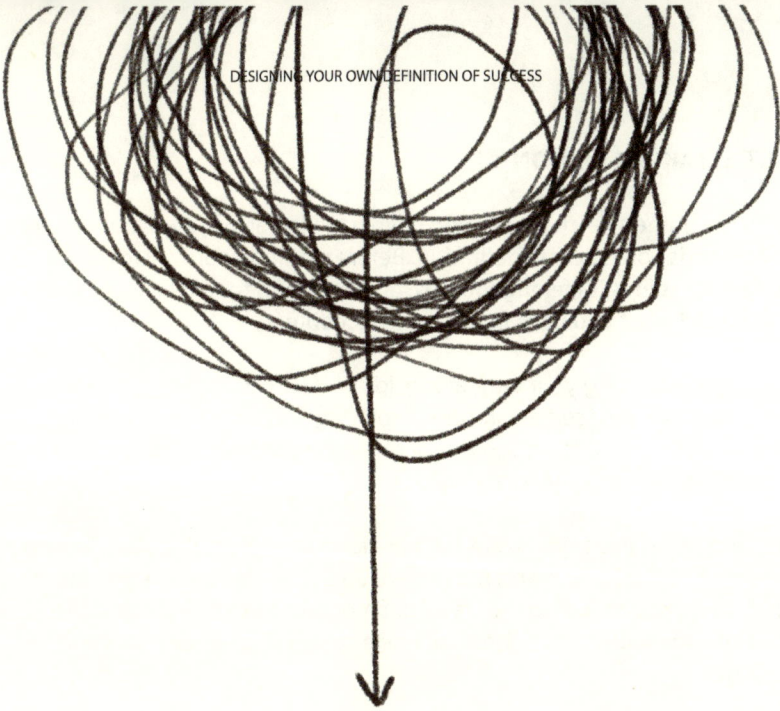

PART 5

TAKING ACTION

PART 5: **TAKING ACTION**

On to the home stretch now… you have travelled an absolute hell of a long way towards your success definition. Before making your way towards the last few steps in this lifelong journey, take a second to reflect, look back, and understand what you have in the past 19 chapters.

From understanding your why, alongside SMART Goals, through to a deep-dive into your self-awareness. Exploring and answering that elusive question *"Who am I?"* through a structured journey through your personality, motivation, learning styles, and values.

You didn't stop there; you went further along to explore the body. Taking control of your nutrition and movement and all-in-all connecting your mind and body. Understanding the details of mental health, how to practise gratitude, managing your stress, all while cultivating mindfulness and resilience.

One hell of a journey!

(Slow clap)

(Slow clap continues…)

Well done.

The only thing left for you to do is to get off your a** and Get. It. Done. Because no one else is going to do it for you. It won't happen naturally. Hope will only get you so far. So it's time to take action!

20

CHAPTER 20: **SUCCESS MINDSET**

It's all well and good to be knowledgeable and learn things theoretically. It means absolutely nothing unless you are willing to take action. So, what makes you take action like there is no tomorrow? Well… what cultivates action is belief. That belief comes from a mindset designed for success – a success mindset.

Action > Belief > Mindset

In today's society, a success mindset is more important than ever before. It gives you the right 'oomph' and the right skills to level up, get shit done, and move towards a successful life – by design. Regardless of whether it's in sports, business, academia, or entertainment; people with a success mindset always seem to figure things out and simply make things happen – regardless of their obstacles or hardships. If you don't believe me, look closer at the lives of successful athletes, entrepreneurs, Hollywood stars *(whoever!)* and their pasts. Every one of these individuals have designed a success mindset regardless of their circumstances, upbringing, or hardships. The beauty is that you can design your own! Let's get on with it right now.

Successful mindset comes down to three different elements:

1.   A growth mindset
2.   Consistent self-reflection and awareness
3.   Positive possibilities

Types of Mindsets

You either have a **fixed** mindset or a **growth** mindset.

Disclaimer: After reading this section, and practising it religiously, you will begin to see everyone around you as having either a growth mindset or a fixed mindset. It will begin to skew your perception of the people around you and distinctly categorise them as fixed or growth. Try not to do that!

To keep things simple, a **growth mindset** is *"the understanding that abilities and understanding can be developed"* – straight from Carol Dweck's book *Mindset* (you will see this in this chapter's Perfect Library design). Those with a growth mindset believe that they can get smarter, more intelligent, and more talented through putting in time and effort.

On the flipside, a **fixed mindset** is one that assumes abilities and understanding are relatively fixed. Those with a fixed mindset may not believe that intelligence can be enhanced, or that you either "have it or you don't" when it comes to abilities and talents.

Let's take a closer look and compare the two mindsets:

Fixed Mindset	Growth Mindset
• Believes intelligence is static • Avoids challenges • Gives up easily when obstacles arise • Sees effort as pointless or worse • Ignores all criticisms/feedback • Feels threatened by the success of others	• Believes intelligence can be developed • Embraces challenges • Never quits when facing obstacles • Sees effort as the pathway to mastery • Takes on board and learns from criticism/feedback • Finds lessons and inspiration in the success of others

A success mindset is a growth mindset.

Consistent self-reflection + self-awareness

This is something we have already covered throughout this book and in part 2. Quite self-explanatory really – it is the ability to look inward at oneself. It is nearly impossible to have a success mindset without self-awareness. This comes with accountability and the ability to look beyond your own ego.

Some important questions to ask yourself are:

* *What did I learn from the situation?*
* *What could I have done?*
* *How can you find the silver lining?*

Mental jiu jitsu!

Consistently asking yourself these questions keeps you humble, looking and moving forward towards one destination: a successful life.

Positive possibilities

This is also called 'optimism'. Not 'blind optimism' – that's just ignorance! This does not mean you all of a sudden believe you can become an astronaut tomorrow, when your whole life you have been a lion tamer! Of course, you can… eventually. But not tomorrow. Maybe after years of consistent hard work. Or maybe you are like me and haven't been blessed with height (I'm 5'7"), but all of a sudden believe you can be the NBA's next slam dunk champion. But in reality, I can embrace the possibility that I can become a relatively good ball player, improve the game, work on the techniques, fitness, all the skills required, and step-by-step, one day become good enough to play for a local team. Then look at advancing. This is my belief. The belief that positive change can happen when you take the necessary steps to make things happen. Exactly like writing this book, or starting my podcast show, my businesses, or anything else in my life.

Guess what? Just like practising your slam dunk technique, a success mindset comes from practice, if you don't already have one. If you believe you can change your outlook *(i.e. you are in the driver's seat)*, then you can start. Start now. Start by figuring out the steps required for you to get to your destination of designing a success mindset. What do you want in your life and how are you going to get there?

In public speaking, this may be setting some goals to speak comfortably and confidently in front of 10 people. You may decide to watch the best speakers in the world, or practice in front of the mirror. Speak in front of the family at first and eventually muster up the courage to speak in front of five people and then eight, then eventually ten. From there, the sky is the limit! Before you know it, you are speaking like a pro in front of 10,000 people. Just like some of my good friends who used to get nervous every single time they spoke, but are now some of the best speakers around Australia and the world.

How to design a Success Mindset

Change your mindset and your life will change.

That's it.

Sounds easy right? Well, that's what most people advise you to do. Whether it's about changing your career, or finding time to learn a new skill, or even something as simple as starting to do push-ups daily. It is a self-fulfilling prophecy – we tell ourselves we can't and these negative words of affirmation form and reinforce our belief system *(almost rewires our brain ready for failure)* and therefore your actions reflect it and you don't do the thing. Therefore, you can't.

How many of us live this pattern? Everyday…

Instead it's as simple as starting with positive words of affirmation such as *"I can"* and *"I will"*. Imagine where your life will be in one month, one year, ten years?

Most importantly: imagine if you don't.

Take a second to let that sink in… can you really afford NOT to tell yourself *"I can"* and *"I will"*?

"

*Everything is created twice,
first in the mind and then in reality.*

Robin Sharma
Best Selling Author

I personally believe *(with every fibre in my body)* that our thoughts and mindset have incredible powers. Everything in our lives – behaviours, ideas, actions, emotions, moods – all stem from how we think. All you have to do is start believing.

"Can you imagine?"

Here are the five hacks that have worked for me in almost every facet of my life:

Growth mindset the hell out of our mind!

If you are telling yourself you are stuck and you have no choices or options in your 'horrible situation' whether in a relationship, work, health, finances… anything. You are most likely stuck in a fixed mindset and guess what? Nothing will change.

However, if you can tell yourself that you can change it, design and create it through specific strategies and focussed actions, then it's simply a matter of walking through those steps. Eventually, you will be where you want to be. It's so obvious which type of people will naturally progress in their lives and grow. Make your self-fulling prophecy is positive one and grow, grow, grow.

Think in abundance

It's called an abundance mentality. Whether it is access to resources, time, energy, money, relationships… everything. BELIEVE there is an abundance of everything in your life. If you feel the opposite, as if you have only a finite amount of the above *(you may be correct)*, but that is a scarcity mentality. This will immediately restrict your growth and hinder your success mainly based on FOMO. #nofomo

If you can recognise this and embrace the very real fact that there is an abundance of everything around you, and accept this whole-heartedly, you are one step closer to a successful life.

Flearning

'Flearning' is failing forward and learning from it. How many of us get paralyzed by the fear of failure? Or won't start something because of the fear of failure?

Well, the reality is that every successful individual, entrepreneur, athlete, speaker, designer, celebrity is simply an accumulated result of their failures with an embraced lifestyle around their failures. They simply fail, learn, and

DESIGNING YOUR OWN DEFINITION OF SUCCESS

move forward.

This does not mean you repeat the same mistake twice. Oh no! The 'learning' in 'Flearning' refers to exactly that.

So, try, fail, learn, try again, fail, and keep trying until you get it right. Does it seem like a lot of work? Well yes, obviously. But if you can fail fast, you can then hack your way to success much faster than originally planned.

Long term – always think and design for long term

How many times have you heard 'overnight success' stories? Probably everywhere you look these days. But the reality is, if you look closely and study the details, you will find out the reality was far from 'overnight'. It is literally years and years of consistent hard work *(growth mindset, abundance mentality, flearning consistently)* that got them to their 'overnight' success.

Hell… Hugh Jackman *(the actor who played and became Wolverine)* used to be a party clown being paid $50/hour. He was probably a damn good clown, but it goes to show that this formula works. Works every single time. Therefore, always plan long term and you will not be disappointed.

Break (some) rules

Anyone who knows me well knows that I am more likely to ask for forgiveness than ask for permission. This approach is not for the faint-hearted because it can land you in some serious trouble sometimes. But again, you learn and move forward. However, despite all the rules I have 'broken', I will endeavour to still 'break rules' where I can, because it makes me a more creative educator, creative speaker, creative designer, and creative businessman.

Risk-averse people will live comfortably in their comfort zone and they have my full respect. Absolutely nothing wrong with that, if that is the life you wish to lead. Breaking *(some)* rules, however, will allow you to challenge the status quo, challenge the system, challenge the industry, and change the world for the better!

(Bit ambitious isn't it?)
(Perhaps… what's wrong with ambition?)

"

I've missed more than 9000 shots in my career.
I've lost almost 300 games.
26 times, I've been trusted to take
the game-winning shot and missed.
I've failed over and over and over again in my life.

And that is why I succeed.

Michael Jordan
Basketball Legend, MVP, GOAT!

"

Know the rules well,
so you can break them effectively.

Dalai Lama XIV
World renowned Buddhist Monk

Design your mindset.

Rashan Senanayake
@rashansenanayake
www.RashanSenanayake.com

CHAPTER SUMMARY: SUCCESS MINDSET
Let's take a look at the key summaries from this chapter:

- **Actions (and their results) lead to your belief and your belief forms your mindset** – make sure it's by design, in a positive direction.
- **Growth mindset with a reflection system combined with positive possibilities** – that's all you need.
- **"I can and I will"** – change your vocabulary to design your life towards success.
- **Embrace an abundant mentality** – there are unlimited resources around and that is the reality and only fact you need to believe.
- **Flearn your way to success** – failure is ok. Take that failure and turn it into a positive by learning from it and moving forward.
- **Think long term** – plan long term and design for long term. Never chase short term success or action towards a short-term gain.
- **Break (some) rules** – ask for forgiveness, not permission. Challenge the status quo and push the boundaries. Combined with flearning, you are on your way to a beautiful success mindset.

THE PERFECT LIBRARY DESIGN
Author's pick for this chapter

- **Mindset: The new psychology of success** - Carol S. Dweck
- **How to Fail** - Elizabeth Day
- **The Squiggly Career** - Helen Tupper & Sarah Ellis

Visit **www.rashansenanayak.com** for the full read list and more resources.

AUDIOBOOK + PODCAST
Extended discussions available on this section, exclusively on Audible.

21

CHAPTER 21: **TIME MANAGEMENT**

86,400 seconds.

1,440 minutes.

24 hours.

1 day.

It is the same for you, same for your family, same for your friends, your competitors, same for me, and it's still the same even if you are Usain Bolt *(the fastest man alive!)*. It is finite and consistent.

We all have the same amount of time in a day. Your success comes down to how you use those 86,400 seconds – every day, day-in and day-out.

In 2024, anyone with a smartphone is averaging one hour a day on social media. Mindless social media. Are you more than that? Or are you less? But on average it is one hour every day. This means it is seven hours every week, twenty-eight hours every month, a total of 364 hours every year. That is fifteen days every year spent on social media. That is seventy-five days over a period of five years! Five years have passed and spending one hour of social media a day has literally wasted two-and-a-half months *(f***ing months!)* on social media.

What could you get done in 2.5 months?

Start a business?

Spend time with your loved ones?

Get healthier?

Learn a new skill?

All of the above?

Perhaps…

So how do the successful athletes, entrepreneurs, and leaders lead an amazing life and get more out of each day? Especially when we have the same amount of time.

Time management.

Time management
Noun

the ability to use one's time effectively or productively.
"time management is the key to efficient working"

But we seem to never ever have enough time in the day. Why? Look closer at how you spend your time. Conduct a time management audit on your life. When designing your pathway to success, one of the most crucial design elements is the use of your time. How you use your time and how you get the most out of each day – by design. It's a learned skill and a planning exercise. All you have to do is follow the steps outlined in this chapter. Simple!

To manage your time to the T, it takes a shift in focus from activities to results: **being productive over being 'busy'. Work smart, not hard.** So, you can get more into less time. More impact in less time. More progress in less time.

What Is Time Management?

Time management is as simple as how you use your time for various activities.

(Isn't it a waste to spend my precious time learning about time management, instead of using it to get on with my work?)

(Well sure! But if you look long term, you will know that spending two to three hours on learning time management will literally uncover years worth of productive time over a period of a decade. So, isn't that worth two to three hours? Maybe even a bit more...)

When you begin to manage your time better, the results speak for themselves. But on top of the results you will also have:

- Greater productivity and efficiency
- A better professional reputation
- Less stress
- Increased opportunities for advancement
- Greater opportunities to achieve important life and career goals

That's just in your professional career.
Outside of your career...

- More time for your health
- More time for your hobbies
- More time for your family and friends
- More time for the things you love (even if that is binge watching your favourite TV show)

On the flipside however, failing to manage your time effectively can lead to:

- Missed deadlines
- Stunted workflow and work satisfaction
- Poor work quality
- A poor professional reputation and a stalled career
- Higher stress levels

Outside of your career...

- Develop unhealthy habits
- No time for enjoyment or hobbies
- Missed relationships

Most importantly, the seconds, minutes, hours, days, months, years that have passed that you will never get back! Never.

(Read that last sentence again. Let it sink in.)

Time, By Design

Unlike everything else in this book, your time is something that will waste away and tick regardless of your life design. Here are some facts for an everyday person:

- 20% of the average workday is spent on "crucial" and "important" things, while 80% of the average workday is spent on things that have "little value" or "no value". The 80/20 rule pops its head up!
- The average person gets one interruption every eight minutes, or approximately seven in an hour, 50–60 per day. The average interruption takes five minutes, making a total of approximately four hours – 50% of the average workday. 80% of those interruptions are typically unimportant, creating approximately three hours of wasted time per day.
- In the last twenty years, working time has increased by 15% and leisure time has decreased by 33%. Why? Read the first two dot points.
- Ten to twelve minutes invested in planning your day will save at least two hours of wasted time and effort throughout the day.

(Whoa!)

Yep, now we are onto something. Plan it. Design it. Build it.

These are some of the strategies that work for me, serve my time, and allow me to make the most of every day, day-in, day-out.

If you invest the next one hour into reading through these strategies, I guarantee that you will be able to find hours that have been lost within each day, and ultimately save days or weeks, or even months, every year!

1.   Know how you spend your time

Have a clear vision. When you have a clear why, the actions you need to take become clearer and therefore you can find out *(and know)* exactly how you want to spend your time. So, the first step is to understand how you already spend your time. Take some notes. Observe. Analyse. How do you spend your time? Sleep? Health? Work? Leisure? Relationship? Play? Life admin? Write it down and ask yourself *"What does my ideal day look like?"* How close are you to your goal?

When you clearly define how you spend your time, you will be better able to keep a record of how you spend your time. There are many apps already out there that can be used to take control and track your time.

Do it.

2.   Prioritise

We don't run out of time. We simply do not make time for something. Day in day out, we can see people all around us that all of a sudden can find the time to do something – remember Jeremy (from Chapter 1)? He could not find fifteen minutes a day to exercise from home for almost eight years. But after Jane (his partner) commented on his appearance at the dinner last week, he is now consistently finding time one hour every two days to exercise and get in shape.

Did Jeremy just unlock a secret that we don't know? Is Jeremy a magician?

Nope, he simply made it a priority above the other items that he had dedicated his time to before Jane's comments about his "soft midsection".

Know your priorities by asking yourself these questions works for me every time:

- Is it urgent or important?
- Does it take me closer or away from my goal at hand?
- Is it necessary?
- What is the result of the activity?
- Can it be delegated?

Practise this and just watch your life transform almost instantly.

3.   Make a to-do list at the end of each day

Some people call me a bit OCD or crazy. But I have a running tracker of every task done to date, over eight years. Every single task, every single detail. This is not something you need; all you need is a simple to-do list at the start of the day (for the day ahead) and a to-do list at the end of the day (for the next day). This gives you a clear vision of exactly what needs to be done. Anything else is not important (urgent matters are of course an exception).

Tip 1: Tag the most important task for the day. Do this first.

Tip 2: Be realistic when scheduling tasks. If something is going to take you five hours, then allocate five hours. Even five and a half hours.

Set yourself up for success.

4.   Focus without distractions

Pause your inbox. Airplane mode your phone. Block social media.

Whatever works for you and whatever is required for you to build healthy and productive work habits.

5.   Time Blocking

As an example, Elon Musk (*only from the point of view him being a well known entrepreneur in the modern world - no speaking of his political choices!*) has the same twenty-four hours in a day that we do. However, he still finds time to lead companies such as SpaceX, Tesla, Solar City (*and more!*). People have repeatedly said he's 'superhuman' when seeing how he manages his time and focus without distractions. However, the secret is simple – time blocking. Time blocking is actually the method of committing a certain number of hours to just one task and blocking off time for other tasks. This method is also detailed over and over again in various books and studies developed by studying successful individuals.

Adjust the time block to suit your life. 15 mins? 45 mins? Design to suit.

6.   Make some decisions

This is not about deciding what is important. You have already done that above through prioritising your tasks. These decisions are about the task at hand. Now it's time to define the task at hand. Ask yourself:

- Which part is of high priority?
- When does this need to be completed?
- Can I fast track the progress through technology, tools, or people?

7.   Tony Robbins' rapid planning method (RPM)

This system (developed by Tony Robbins) is a results-focused planning system to change your mindset to concentrate more on the end outcome. Rapid planning method (RPM) stands for:

- R - Result-oriented
- P - Purpose-driven

- M - Massive-action plan

These three portions help in getting better answers to focus our efforts in a better way.

8.   Record your daily routine

This is the feedback system that will allow you to refine and iterate your time management strategies by being able to find out how your time is used. Use a productivity app, write it down, use a calendar – anything. But make a record that allows you to understand how your time is used and identify where time is wasted.

Your next iteration can then refine these 'defects'.

9.   Automate your workflow

Can the tasks you do repetitively be automated?

Life admin, business admin, tracking, recording – anything. Use technology to automate various tasks and save your time for better things.

It took me four years until I actively did this! Four years I will never get back which held countless hours wasted on repetitive tasks. Don't make the same mistake.

10.   Be organised

It's a decision. It's not a born trait or genetics. Get organised. As you would organise the files in your computer by putting them into various folders – do the same with your life. Categorise the various tasks – i.e. work, personal, health, family, friends, etc.

This will naturally allow you to feel more organised and tackle activities, tasks, and work more cohesively and manage your time easier.

11.   Do the MITs first!

*(Did you mean go to MIT?) No… *Facepalm*.*

This strategy is about doing the Most Important Tasks (MIT) first thing in the morning from your to-do list. This will not only rewire your brain every morning for success by pumping your brain with happy juice and endorphins from completing a task, it will keep you hooked day in day out, looking for the same 'fix'.

Well it works. When you complete the MITs first, it reduces the stress for the day ahead (early on) and allows you to do more each day with the newfound energy.

Be careful though… it is addictive.

## 12.	Batch, batch, and batch.

Are there small tasks that you have to do often? Like reply to emails, finances, life admin, laundry, cooking. Well, batch them.

Let's take a small example: cooking. It may take you ten minutes to set up for cooking and twenty minutes for clean up after every cooking session. This means that if you cook five times a week, you are spending fifty minutes on set up and a hundred minutes on clean up. However, if you cook once *(or twice)*, your set up time is the same *(ten minutes)* and your clean up may increase a tad *(due to the larger task)* – say thirty minutes. Just like that, within a week you have saved 110 minutes simply by batching your cooking!

Replying to emails is the same, but is a more frequent activity. Not to mention the loss of focus on the task at hand and the energy your brain requires to re-focus after checking your inbox. Batching can not only save you time, but also allow you to fast-track your goals, increase your focus, and conserve energy. Simple.

## 13.	Perfectionism is not productive

If you are searching for perfection, then you are in for a long wait! Especially if you think of it as a strength for yourself! But ask yourself one question: has any successful person *(ever!)* been perfect right from the start?

(If you didn't guess already – the answer is 'no'.)

So don't let your strive to be perfect – whether in your eyes or others – make you waste your precious time. Simply do what is important, right now, right here.

## 14.	Just say "NO"

This is not for the faint-hearted. Because you will piss off people – it's the reality. People do not like being told no, or being denied control.

One of the nicknames placed on me in the past has been "Mr. No". Why? Well, because I would say no to things that would be a waste of time.

(Looking back now, it has a cool ring to it. Kind of like a James Bond villain!)

But the power of saying no – stemming from a clear vision – is so powerful in managing your time effectively. This may even be small distractions that occur in your workplace every day: simply say no. If your to-do list is already full and you receive a request to complete an additional task on the same day, decline it. Don't agree to work on a task or help a colleague until you have the time to do so. Keep your priorities straight and simple.

Because if you say yes when you cannot, you will only end up disappointing your colleague, boss, and even yourself, not to mention your own self-esteem.

15. Design in your breaks and 'R n' R'

Whether it's ten to fifteen minute breaks between meetings or completing tasks, make sure your schedule is designed with these in place. Do not compromise these to simply fit more in. You want to make the most effective use of your time within a day, and that's why you jump from one task to the next without wasting any time in between. Now, this might look like a good use of your time at first sight, but eventually it proves to be the exact opposite. That is, being busy, and not being productive.

Make time to Rest and Recuperate (R n' R).

After all, the human brain needs a break after every ninety minutes in order to maintain the highest levels of concentration and motivation.

So, to manage your time effectively – design in your breaks.

16. Don't half-ass it!

It's easy to get lost between what we should be doing and what others want us to do. For example, you're working on a task from your to-do list, but you stop randomly to work on a report that your boss asked for. This is what we call 'half-work'. No matter how or where you encounter half-work, the result is the same: poor commitments, poor engagement, poor performance – half assed! Congratulations…

This is a combination of prioritising + saying no + time blocking.

17. "Let's outsource it"

Your time is finite. But your resources are in abundance (abundance mentality). Therefore, if you can leverage your resources, technology, team members, or even other people, then delegating and outsourcing the simple stuff means you are creating many workflows for the same goal. You are bound to reach the goal faster by delegation.

Delegation Tip: Make sure that you hand over the responsibilities to the right person, with the right skills. Otherwise it is not going to serve your life productively – it will in fact take you further away from your goals and waste more time.

18.   Just STOP multitasking

They say women can multitask better than men. Perhaps. But the reality is in fact that no one should (and can productively) multitask. A recent psychological study showed that people who prefer to practise the habit of multitasking find it difficult to concentrate and maintain focus on work when needed *(google it)*. Most of them believe that routine multitasking helps to save time and accomplish more in a day, but in reality, it's literally the opposite. Most of the work is half-assed, or if the work is at a high quality, the individual will be drained and feel overworked and head towards burnout quickly.

Be present. Focus on the single task at hand. You have all the upside.

19.   Design, re-design, and iterate

Just like any other design activity, design and iterate your time management strategies *(if you have any)* and constantly refine it. Spend five minutes once a week to refine the week ahead. How can you gain more from your peak performance times? How can you increase your relaxation time? Are you feeling overworked? If so, where can improvements be made?

Refine it. Consistently.

21.   Use the tools at your disposal

Do you think you can remember everything? Well, good for you. It may be working now, but it is difficult to scale your life or even keep that as a sustainable lifestyle. Use the tools and technology at your disposal to leverage your time back. Keep it as a record, schedule things easier, remove human error, control the timing, set reminders, and make yourself available as you wish – by design.

(I don't have access to technology.)

(Use a calendar.)

(I don't have access to a calendar.)

(Draw a calendar.)

(I don't have access to drawing equipment.)

(Scratch it on the wall.)

(I don't…) (Stop making excuses!)

22.   Don't waste time waiting

Whether you are waiting for a friend who has no respect for your time, waiting for your coffee, waiting for your teammates to finish their tasks, waiting for your… anything. Consider adding more value to your life. Listen to an audiobook, podcast, research your side-hustle, do some push-ups. Add more value to your life.

This will help you consistently grow and develop, ready to get back to the task when the other variables have come through and you have effectively taken a break as well!

Win-win.

You are welcome!

All you have to do is now design the 86,400 seconds you have every day.

Design towards using the time you have,
or you will lose it forever,
in every second passed.

Rashan Senanayake
@rashansenanayake
www.RashanSenanayake.com

CHAPTER SUMMARY: TIME MANAGEMENT
Let's take a look at the key summaries from this chapter:

- **Time is finite** – but what you do with it is your decision entirely. The proof is all around you.
- **Design your time management strategy** – take control, record it, refine it, iterate it, and implement it.
- **Use tools, technology and people to your advantage and get more done.**
- **Time blocking works** – adjust to suit your lifestyle and context.
- **Focus and stay focused** – remove the distractions and build in breaks to work towards your goals.
- **Do it right now** – or it will be too late.

THE PERFECT LIBRARY DESIGN
Author's pick for this chapter

- **Deep work** - Cal Newport
- **The 4-hour Work Week** - Tim Ferriss
- **168 Hours: You Have More time than you think** - Laura Vanderkam
- **The 80-20 Principle** - Richard Koch

Visit **www.rashansenanayak.com** for the full read list and more resources.

AUDIOBOOK + PODCAST
Extended discussions available on this section, exclusively on Audible.

22

CHAPTER 22: **HABITS FOR SUCCESS**

This is what it all comes down to. The glue. The anchor. The final piece of the puzzle.

habit
Noun

A settled or regular tendency or practice, especially one that is hard to give up.
"he has an annoying habit of interrupting me"

So, what exactly is a habit? Well let me ask you this… when you brush your teeth, which side do you start from? Left? Right? Top left? Bottom left? You know what… it really doesn't matter! Most of us will be starting from the same place, every single time. Because it is our habit to do so.

What about the first thing you do when you walk in the door after work?

What about the snacks we eat?

Work practices?

Social media use?

Actions just before bed?

How about our emotional reactions?

How you treat your family?

Habits. All habits. Things we do on autopilot without a thought, our inclinations, tendencies… they are all habits. It happens with very little conscious thought on your part. Which ultimately means that you are spending less energy on decision making. Things simply happen.
This is a double-edged sword!

If you are doing positive practices as a habit, then it can only mean that you are going to go from strength to strength. In the same light, if you have destructive habits, then it's only a matter of time until you are going to find yourself in a negative and difficult place.

Scientists have learned that a certain part of the brain called the 'basal ganglia' plays a crucial role in creating new habits and maintaining existing ones. This leads us to understand why some people, even after major brain damage, will still do certain things they've always done before, like find their way home without any conscious previous recollection of where they are going. These people often don't even know how or why they can still do certain things, but if the basal ganglia is intact, those old habits are still available. The latest research also shows that habits are so ingrained in our brains that we keep acting in accordance with them, even when we no longer benefit from them.

Researchers from Duke University have shown that over 40% of what we do is determined not by decisions but by habits. This suggests that we can change a huge part of our lives just by eliminating bad habits and creating good ones instead. People who fully understand this have been able to find wonderful new ways to change their lives for the better.

How are habits formed?

Let's go with a coffee example *(because it is now a habit of mine – a habit that didn't exist till 2019)*. Maybe you take a train to work, and automatically buy a coffee while you wait for your train. This habit will have formed in the following way:

At the start it requires conscious thought. Seeing the coffee stand, a friend speaking positively about drinking coffee *(essentially what happened to me),* and then the rest is history!

(What happens next?)

- Deciding that you would like a coffee
- Going to the coffee stand and buying a coffee
- Drinking your coffee on the train
- Repeat the next day, and the next, and the next

(So?)

You are forming associations and triggers to allow your habit to develop. Develop without you even realising. Over time you associate arriving at the station with getting a coffee. The trigger can be the station or seeing the coffee stand.

For a habit to stick, usually you have to derive some sort of pleasure from it for the habit to continue to strengthen. This might be liking the coffee taste, the warmth of the cup in your head, the hit you get from the caffeine, the social acceptance, filler conversation – anything positive!
What have you done? You have set up:

- Trigger to fire the habit
- Association with a reward

That's it. You are hooked. A coffee addict. Just like a crack addict… you grab a coffee every morning without having to think about it. But one morning you are late because the habit may be so strong that you missed your train, as you had to have your coffee. Or you are on the train, thinking about how to get your morning coffee when you get off. A year later you cannot even function – or feel empty – without your caffeine hit in the morning.

You are now the proud owner of a coffee habit!

(So? What's the big deal!)

Well, there is an important lesson here for you: as the designer of your own life, you can set up triggers and reward loops to create positive habits – success habits.

Success habits of the successful

This is not rocket science. There are distinct patterns, behaviours, and attributes that the *(people that society deems)* successful practice. All you have to do is spend your time studying this, and observe the successful entrepreneurs, CEOs, athletes, thought leaders, or even A-grade students in primary schools.

But since today is a lucky day, I have done that work for you and outlined all the success habits these types of individuals practise with a disciplined approach! Here we go…

Read about your industry – immerse yourself in the subject matter

Warren Buffett *(the investment king of the world)* is known to read six hours every day! Buffet has been doing this consistently for *(literally!)* decades of his journey to become a thought leader of your industry. Now this doesn't mean you have to go and read six hours every day! All you need is thirty minutes a day *(minimum)*. That is three-and-a-half hours every week. That is fourteen hours every month. 168 hours every year. That is equivalent to one week of your year spending time reading, non-stop. If you do sixty minutes every day, that is two weeks of every year!

Imagine the sheer amount of knowledge you will gain by adding drops of knowledge to your bucket consistently. Eventually there will be no one in the world who knows better that you, on that particular topic! This is how you become a thought-leader in your industry.

Keep a daily journal or a tracker

It's simply a record of your life. Easy. *(Why?)* Well… good question. The reason is that it helps you visualise, keep yourself accountable, measure and track progress, and design what you need to do based on where you want to be – your success definition!

It is your feedback loop. Accountability is the big idea here, to ensure you take action and understand why you're doing so.

Pump that iron

This doesn't mean go on to be a bodybuilder. Successful individuals ALL – not one or two, not half, ALL – have a specific physical regime. This not only gives you more energy, but also designs your mental fitness. Strong body. Strong mind.

Be courageous

Sometimes it's also known as 'no fear'. What it actually means is that you are managing any fears through courageous actions. Being fearless will always open doors and allow you to step up to the plate and face anything that is staring you down, courageously.

Unplug regularly

Every successful individual always makes sure they unplug daily – without a device. No phone, no internet, no TV, no screen, no tablet. A book, your partner, family, outdoors, pets, loved ones, or simply yourself. This allows you to successfully recharge and reset to tackle bigger and better challenges.

No ego

Ego is your enemy. Ego will turn others into your enemy. Great leaders, and all successful individuals who maintain that success are always grounded, humble and down to earth – genuinely. People naturally gravitate towards this if you can check your ego at the door, every day!

No quitting

Never give up. Be relentless.

If you never quit, you can never be a failure. It is only a matter of time until you are successful.

Inspired circle

This is a habit. It's a choice.

To be successful, you have to surround yourself with like minded individuals. Successful individuals do not spend their energy worrying about, or even interacting with the keyboard warriors that troll your posts on social media.

Understand that negativity generally comes from unhappy people and those who envy you. Happy successful people don't tear others down – it is usually a reflection of themselves, rather than you. Surround yourself with ambitious, positive people. You will become the sum of the five closest people you surround yourself with. It's too easy to focus on the negative and there's just no upside to that. Make it a habit to design and surround yourself with #**inspired** individuals.

Listen and learn

Listen. Listen and listen some more. There is a reason that evolution has gifted us with two ears and only one mouth. Listen and learn. Listen to your colleagues, family, podcasts, audiobooks, news, mentors, unhappy customers, your critics, haters. Listen to everyone – but learn. Learn from the nuggets of gold that are hidden behind everything you listen to.

Make sure that whatever you listen to and the information that goes into your brain is positive. Words and sounds that inspire you. That make you level up and grow.

Being organised is a priority

Making lists and setting daily goals helps you stay focused each day. There are so many fires to put out each day, so being organised helps you stay task-oriented and helps you stay on track and meet your goals. You should have planning meetings to map out your vision and goals for the next six and twelve months. This helps you focus on the big picture of growing a new business and measuring your successes and failures over time.

Become detail oriented

Don't half-ass things and call it a personality trait. That is simple BS that people use to excuse themselves from doing things half-assed. Successful individuals don't have time or value for that. Become detail-oriented. The difference in grades, the customer service, the mere millimetres by which you may win the race *(unless you are Usain Bolt!)* are all in the details.

Balanced lifestyle

It's funny how all successful individuals have a balanced lifestyle *(or aspire to and are working towards a balanced lifestyle)* but are consistently refining it. Successful does not mean working twenty hours a day. It does not mean working two hours a day. It means finding value in your work and doing the work required while looking after yourself, developing positive relationships, enjoying your day in the present moment, growing… day by day.

Be grateful and practice gratitude

Success is never tied to how much money you have in your bank. Therefore, it encompasses many different types of wealth. Financial wealth, time wealth, health wealth… successful individuals are extremely grateful and consistently practise gratitude for what they have today. While working towards bigger and better goals.

To make an impact, make sure to write it down. Reflect on it. Rewire your brain chemistry towards a successful life.

Learn to say NO!

Only to things that are a distraction from your priorities. Maybe if you cannot say 'no', it's better to say 'not right now' and prioritise the goals at hand. Revisit that opportunity later. Never give in to the fear of missing out, because as we have discussed earlier, an abundant mentality will pave the pathway to more opportunities as you progress.

Be and live only in the present

There is a reason it is called the 'present'. It is a gift. It is right now, right here. The past is gone and cannot be changed, and the future is yet to come, and can be designed – right here, right now. Therefore, your action and focus is to be present and live in the present moment.

Start the day with a win

Your day ahead might be filled with a lot of difficult tasks and challenges to overcome. Or it might be a complete breeze and have essentially nothing planned. Either way – give yourself an endorphin release and some oxytocin release by smashing small tasks such as twenty-five pushups, making your bed, a quick ten minute task. That win will set up the rest of your day – each day. Whatever happens, you've then achieved something that day.

Plan and prepare on Sunday

I learned to plan for the week ahead on each Sunday from fifth grade. Why? It made the entire week a breeze. I was prepared, and ready. Similarly, in primary school, through to high school, university, work life, in business, in sports, in anything – Sundays allow you to take a break and prepare yourself for the week ahead, mentally, physically and environmentally.

No Sunday night plans

Building on the previous success habit, Sunday nights are reserved for family, at home, recuperation and relaxation only. Nothing else, nothing more. Don't even do too many chores! Especially if your week ahead is a hectic one.

List your improvement goals

I keep a running list of goals for improvement written on a digital note. It makes me more conscious of where I can do better. These may be fine-tuning my public speaking, writing this book, business goals, personal goals, financial goals, relationship goals, health goals – anything.

Walk during your phone calls

Taking a brisk walk around the house, block, office, floor during your phone calls is the best hack to combine your professional goals with your health goals – the easiest way is to make those steps so your Apple Watch can congratulate you on meeting your daily standing and walking requirements.

Meditate

(Ohhhhhhhhhhhhhhhhhhhhhmmmmmmmmmmm.)

There are more ways to meditate than simply sitting and chanting *"Ohhhm"*. Meditation is about letting go of all elements and accepting the present moment for what it is. Focusing on your breathing for just ten to fifteen minutes in the morning gets you into a mindset where you're better able to step back from the thoughts and emotions that might cloud your thinking. Through mindfulness, you are able to approach situations with much more clarity to better focus on what's really important and prioritise your time accordingly, both professionally and personally.

Find a natural connection

Walk in the park? Ten minutes of morning Vitamin D intake? Bike ride? Gardening? Whatever works for you, find a connection to nature.

Play some music!

Let music influence your emotions and mood. Just like right now – I am listening to my 'Success' playlist as I write this very sentence. Music is powerful and can unlock energy and emotions that can drive you successfully towards any goal. Even in the car, blast the A-list playlist that gets you ready to take on a charging rhino! The only downside is that it gets a bit awkward at a red light when you catch the next car staring at you while you're belting out the words to Katy Perry's Roar *(Or Eye of the Tiger!)*.

But listen to music every day. Success habits can also be enjoyable.

Keep calm

When in doubt, keep calm. It is the best thing in any situation – good or bad. Create a calming environment by design.

Find your R n' R time

Make it a priority and find time to relax, rest, and recoup. Take an hour at the end of every day to decompress and unwind. Not only will you get to relieve the day's stress, but you'll give yourself the chance to really absorb everything you learned during the day and evaluate your next steps. Entrepreneurs tend to be workaholics *(so they say!)*, but it's important to take a break from the grind and hustle and let yourself breathe. Your business can only be in good shape if you are too.

Visualise your future

Increase productivity by allowing yourself to focus on the task at hand. An effective way to do this is by splitting your time into two categories: 1) Telling yourself what to do, and 2) Doing what you tell yourself to do. I use my calendar, email, and a to-do list on the wall to tell future me what to work on. Before the end of every day, I make sure it's updated so that when I get to my office in the morning, I know exactly what I need to do.

Get #inspired by reading something inspiring.

Like this book. So, you can cross that off the list already!

But once you are done with this book, move onto the perfect library design and get crackin'.

Move

Literally move. Move your body – whether it's taking time to work out or a quick walk around the block after lunch. Anything, but be consistent.

Never quit

Absolutely refuse to quit on anything in your life – your goals, your health, your career, your relationship, your personal development.

The key to these success habits lies in its consistency and proactive action. So how can you make it stick? Make sure it never goes away? Well, it's easier said than done. But it can be done!

There are many components to this:

- **How to design success habits** – this is obvious now that we have outlined what they are!
- **How to unlearn a bad habit** – because most of the time, that's what gets in the way.
- **How to make success habits stick** – the final nail in the coffin! So to say…

How to design success habits

1. Identify and analyse

Ask yourself: What are your goals within your definition of success?

This is a very difficult question to answer because most of the time we do not know exactly what we want. Which is why clarity on your 'why' (discussed in Chapter 1) will shine more light on exactly what habits will design the success definition you want.

Is it a health habit? Maybe you want to be able to walk uphill next to your friends and not have to stop to catch your breath? Relationship habit? Maybe you want to be able to spice things up with your partner? Financial habit? Maybe you want to save some dollars to enter the property market? Whatever it might be, ask yourself, *"What are your goals within your definition of success?"*

From here, analyse the cause and effect of your current habit. i.e. Why don't you have enough money to enter the property market? Is it because of your earnings? Spending habits? Expenses/bills? Perhaps all the above? Well, now you will be able to see where unwanted spending habits are placed and refine your habit. Later in this chapter, we will be going through exactly how to make a new success habit work and make it stick. Do the same with all attributes of your life.

What are your goals within your definition of success? > Analyse the cause and effect of the current context > Write down what you need to do to design towards your goal (i.e. a success habit)

2. Rinse n' repeat

Do this same process with all your goals and derive a change map based on your current habits.

One step closer… now it's time to get rid of the bad habits to make way for the success habits that you have designed – aimed directly at the bullseye that is your own definition of success!

How to unlearn a bad habit

An essential part of creating success habits is getting rid of the bad habits that we have learned consciously and unconsciously. We are all guilty of learning bad habits… most of the time! We all grab for our favourite snack when we are feeling lazy – even when we are not hungry. Go window shopping and end up spending a couple of hundred dollars… just because. Even choose to watch Netflix instead of working on that passion project.

Why? We may know that our actions are working against us and taking us further away from our own definition of success. But yet, we do it day-in and day-out – almost like there is a force that is bigger than us making us do it automatically!

Absolutely bullsh*t! That is only an excuse we give ourselves so we can avoid a difficult conversation.

But of course, you are different! You are the minority that wants to design your life towards your own success goals. So, let's get rid of those bad habits – consciously!

1.   Identify

Categorise your life into the various elements – health, finances, relationship, career, etc. *(up to you!)*. Then carry out a thorough audit and ask yourself *"What are the bad habits here?"* within each element. Write it down.

2.   Avoid & Replace & Reward

To get rid of a bad habit, you cannot simply depend on willpower. We all need to consciously avoid it (i.e. side-step all possible triggers) and replace it with a good habit. Always replace it with a good habit – or even a small habit that pulls you in the right direction. Finally, reward yourself for doing the good habit.

For example, if you are wanting to cut down your mindless social media habits you may:

- **Avoid** by: keeping your phone in the next room for one hour at first (then extending the time)

- **Replace** by: doing push-ups every time you get the urge to check social media for no apparent reason
- **Reward** by: buying that book for your perfect library design!

Give yourself a few days and watch your mental and physical health improve, while designing new and amazing habits that kick goals for your life!

3.   Lay one brick at a time

Good work! The hard part is done… now it's a matter of doing it one day at a time. Focus on the present. Avoid, replace, reward. Avoid, replace, reward. Avoid, replace, reward. As Will Smith says: lay one brick at a time and lay that brick as best as you can. Soon you will have built an entire wall, and not long after, a whole house!

Although it changes from person to person, there are many studies that show a habit will begin to stick after repeating it for twenty-one days and it will become a lifetime practice after ninety days. Change these numbers to suit yourself through your heightened self-awareness now that you are following the practices outlined earlier in this book! *Wink*

4.   Track it!

Finally, track everything! The days, the results, your reactions – everything. This will allow you to design success habits easier and easier while refining the ones you are already building.

Almost there… now let's make it stick!

How to make success habits stick

Wouldn't it be nice to have everything run on autopilot? Chores, exercise, eating healthily, and getting your work done all just happening automatically. Well… unless they manage to invent robot servants, all your work isn't going to disappear overnight. But if you program behaviours as new habits, you can take out the struggle. Habits make things happen automatically… even if it's hard to get them established.

With a small amount of initial discipline, a specific design plan – all cultivated from each of the topics discussed so far – you can create new habits… success habits that walk you day by day towards your own definition of a successful life.

Here are the actionable tips for you to make your success habits stick:

Commit to Thirty Days

As a rule of thumb, thirty days (30) was the number of days I used to make adjustments as I want. But three to four weeks is all the time you need to make a habit automatic. If you can make it through the initial conditioning phase, it becomes much easier to make it stick. A month is a good block of time to commit to a change since it easily fits in your calendar. Do it consciously, and don't stop after a few days like the majority.

Do it Daily. Be Consistent.

Consistency is the key if you want to make a habit stick. If you want to start exercising, go to the gym every day for your first thirty days *(don't workout super hard on your first day so you become sore for the rest of the month!)*.

Start Simple

Don't try to completely change your life in one day, or workout so hard that you are trying to force that six pack to show up on day one. Abs don't show up on day one, or day two, or even day seven. Do it for a month and they will begin to surface. It is easy to get over-motivated and take on too much. If you want to study two hours a day, first make the habit to go for thirty minutes, then build on that. Chip away at it like a master builder and turn that log into a beautiful work of art – that is you.

Set Reminders

Around two weeks into your commitment it can be easy to forget your why. Place reminders to execute your habit each day or you might miss a few days and forget why you are doing it.

Get a Buddy

Find yourself an accountability partner who can keep you on track. Make sure this person is either on the same journey as you *(so that you can motivate each other)* or has done it themselves! Don't get yourself a hypocrite as an accountability partner – that is a sure-fire way to set yourself up for failure.

Design Your Trigger

A trigger is a ritual you use right before executing your habit. For example, my trigger for gyming is to prepare my post-workout protein shake – this is automatic for me. However, what then follows is also now automatic, which is to workout two or three times a week. Set up easy triggers that allow you to simply start and get you into the flow towards your habit.

Remove the Sh*t, But Replace the Need

If you are giving up a bad habit, make sure you are replacing any needs you've lost. If watching television gives you a way to relax, you could take up meditation or reading as a way to replace that same need. Make sure the need is replaced.

Be Imperfect

Perfect doesn't exist. Expect the your attempt to set up success habits will fail. It took me about four years of different attempts before I started exercising regularly – now a life without a workout is not a life worth living! Never quit, and expect a few road bumps and falls along the way – that's the beauty of it. It's ok to not get it perfectly nailed on the first attempt.

Affirm Yourself

Be your biggest fan. Even if everyone around you is telling you to stop or try something else – stick to your goals and habits, because you know exactly why you're doing them. So learn to back yourself. *"I may not have achieved this yet, but I definitely know I will down the track".*

("You got this! Go for gold!") Just some of the weird things I tell myself...

Remove Temptation

If you want to stop eating it. Don't buy it. Walk away from the aisle. Don't even make eye contact and avoid it like they said something about your mother! *(I do this with Arnotts TeeVee snacks)*. Restructure your environment so it won't tempt you – especially in the first thirty days.

Surround Yourself With Role Models

Spend more time with people who model the habits you want to mirror. Want to become a professional tennis player? Well you are not going to be a tennis player hanging around with librarians! Go and find professional tennis players. If you can't find professional ones just yet, find people who simply just play tennis. A recent study found that having an obese friend indicated you were more likely to become overweight in the coming year. You become what you spend time around.

An eagle hanging around with chickens will eventually begin to think of itself as a chicken, and even avoid taking flight and soaring the sky.

Experiment

No, this is not the 'experimenting' that you are thinking of...

Withhold judgement until after a month has passed, and use it as an experiment in behaviour. Experiments can't fail, they just have different results, so it will give you a different perspective on changing your habit. Then you can redefine, redesign, and iterate towards your goal. One step closer.

Write it Down

There is a power in the written word. There is a power to putting pen to paper and spelling out what you are doing and trying to achieve. Writing makes your ideas clearer and focuses you on your end result.

Know and Believe Your Why

Be crystal clear on why you are doing what you are doing. Familiarise yourself with the benefits of making this change. Read books that show the benefits of regular exercise. Notice any changes in energy levels after you take on a new diet. Imagine getting better grades after improving your study habits. Connect it with your why and the outlying benefits until eventually doing anything else seems utterly stupid!

Visualise the Flip Side

What happens if you don't do it? You should also be aware of the consequences. Exposing yourself to realistic information about the downsides of not making this change will give you added motivation.

Do it For Your Future Self

Don't worry about all the things you 'should' have as habits. Instead, use your habits towards your goals and the things that motivate you. If your future self (one year from now, five years from now, ten years from now, twenty years from now) would come and see you right now – what would they tell you? Don't build a life that will make your future self kick your current self's ass! Build success habits that will make your future self thank your current self.

That's it. It's just a lifelong journey, a continuous design process and a commitment to yourself to **design your own definition of success.**

Now it's time to take action. Right now.

CHAPTER SUMMARY: HABITS FOR SUCCESS

Let's take a look at the key summaries from this chapter:

- **A habit is a settled or regular tendency or practice** – Especially one that is hard to give up.
- **All successful people have a common pattern: their success habits** – Emulate what has already worked for all types of successful individuals and *design* those habits to become your own tailored version.
- **Habits are formed consciously and unconsciously** – Design your habits consciously.
- **Identify, analyse, and rinse n' repeat** – Design the habits that will take you closer to your definition of success.
- **Unlearning bad habits is a part of designing your success habits** – You cannot learn new habits until you can let go of bad habits. Be open to unlearning and relearning the success habits.
- **Plan for success and make it stick** – Follow all the actionable tips to make sure the new success habit you are designing will become a habit that sticks.
- **Now is the time to take action** – You have all the tools required to design your own definition of success.

THE PERFECT LIBRARY DESIGN

Author's pick for this chapter

- **Atomic Habits** - James Clear
- **The Power of Habit** - Charles Duhigg
- **Daily Rituals: How Artists Work** - Mason Currey

Visit **www.rashansenanayak.com** for the full read list and more resources.

AUDIOBOOK + PODCAST

Extended discussions available on this section, exclusively on Audible.

True Happiness is Success.

Rashan Senanayake
@rashansenanayake
www.RashanSenanayake.com

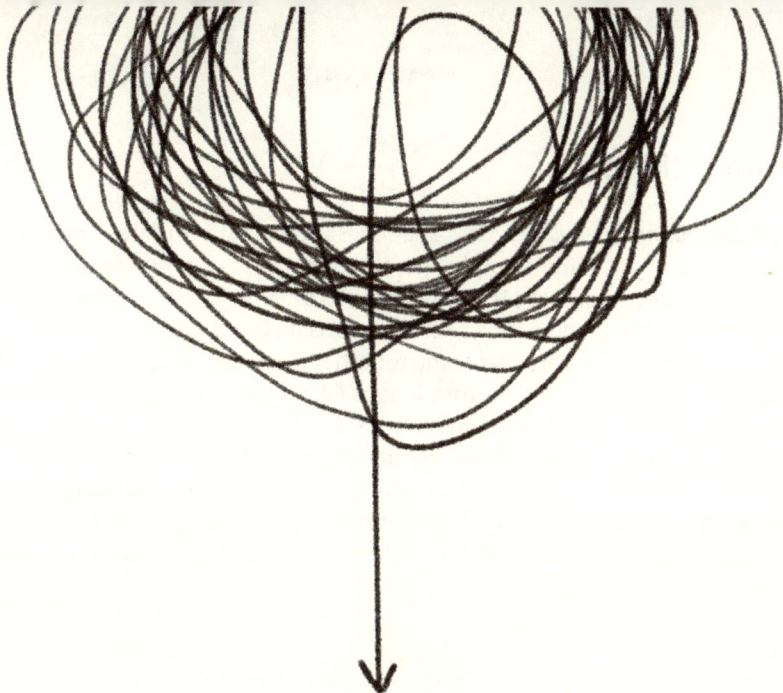

A REASON FOR BEING

IKIGAI

DESIGNING YOUR OWN DEFINITION OF SUCCESS

What is Ikigai?

Ikigai (*pronounced "ee-key-guy"*) is a Japanese term that translates roughly to "*reason for being*" or, more simply, "the thing that gets you out of bed in the morning." It's about finding the perfect blend of what you love, what you're good at, what the world needs, and what you can be paid for—four distinct but interconnected pillars that come together to create a deeply personal sense of purpose. Originating from Japan's Okinawa region, known for its high life expectancy and sense of community, Ikigai has been a guiding philosophy for many people for centuries. It's about finding joy and satisfaction in the everyday while still holding onto long-term goals, making it both inspiring and very practical. And it's the perfect way to add fullness and texture to the (honestly pretty dry sometimes) task of finding your why and planning your SMART goals.

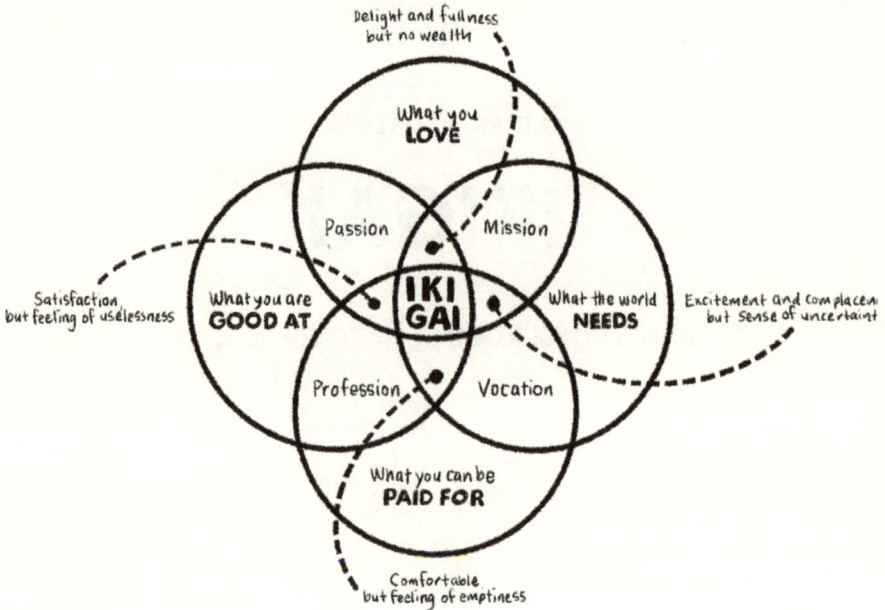

Delight and fullness but no wealth

What you **LOVE**

Passion

Mission

Satisfaction but feeling of uselessness

What you are **GOOD AT**

IKIGAI

What the world **NEEDS**

Excitement and complacent but sense of uncertainty

Profession

Vocation

What you can be **PAID FOR**

Comfortable but feeling of emptiness

The Four Pillars of Ikigai

Ikigai is represented as an overlapping Venn diagram of four circles (which you can find below), with each of the circles representing a key pillar:

1. **What You Love** – This is your passion, the things you find joy in and look forward to.
2. **What You're Good At** – This pillar encompasses your skills, talents, and strengths. Think of it as your unique offering.

3. **What the World Needs** – Here, you're tapping into ways you can make a meaningful impact on others or on society.
4. **What You Can Be Paid For** – This is your financial anchor, the way you can sustain yourself through work. It's separate from the others because sometimes it doesn't fully match! But if there's at least some overlap, you can sustain yourself.

Where all four circles overlap, you'll find your Ikigai. In Japan, having an Ikigai has long been associated with mental well-being, longevity, and a fulfilling life. This isn't about a fast-track to wealth or status; instead, it's about creating a life that feels valuable and meaningful, regardless of what's trending or externally expected.

Why Does Ikigai Matter Today?

Finding purpose can feel elusive, especially when you're at a crossroads in life like starting university or a new job. We often spend more time "doing" than "being," driven by external pressures rather than our inner motivations. This is where Ikigai has helped me today, acting as a compass in my hectic life. Integrating Ikigai into your life encourages a shift toward a more balanced, holistic, and inspired existence. Instead of prioritising work over personal values or vice versa, you're encouraged to make career and life choices that bring you a sense of fulfilment and joy in a rounded way.

A purposeful life, centred on an Ikigai, enables a healthier work-life blend. The key, though, is to check in with your Ikigai regularly (I like to meditate, but I know a lot of people prefer journaling – just find what works for you!). By always revisiting what drives you, you can avoid burnout and even contribute more meaningfully to the world around you. It's a grounding framework for personal and professional fulfilment that allows you to fluidly adapt to life's changes while staying connected to what matters to you.

Designing a Purposeful Career Using Ikigai

Ikigai offers a strong foundation for authenticity and fulfilment when designing a career that aligns with your why. Instead of focusing purely on traditional career markers, like promotions or pay raises, Ikigai (plus the other tools we've discussed) helps you set goals that genuinely resonate. By aligning your career path with your Ikigai, you're able to create a roadmap for ongoing growth, where learning and curiosity play just as big a role as financial accomplishment.

Start by mapping your skills and interests against the four pillars of Ikigai. Ask yourself what parts of your work you truly love, where you excel, and how your work contributes to other people's lives. Think about how your current career aligns with these values. From here, you can establish a development plan, setting goals for continuous learning that align with what's meaningful to you, rather than just ticking off the list of professional achievements that your society or family gave you.

Society often has a set path it expects us to follow—study, get a job, succeed, save, retire—but Ikigai invites us to re-examine that journey. Overcoming these challenges requires resilience and a willingness to carve out your own path. Financial worries, for instance, are a common obstacle when pursuing purpose-driven work, but a balanced Ikigai approach reminds us to stay rooted while still looking ahead, while SMART goals help us find new ways to work around the pressure until we meet the success we want.

With Ikigai as your guide, you can learn to embrace these challenges for what they really can be: opportunities for growth. Building resilience means staying adaptable, not just through success but also through setbacks, and letting these experiences refine your life (and career) vision over time.

Discovering Your Ikigai

Let's get started! This activity will help you identify and align the four key elements of Ikigai—what you love, what you are good at, what the world needs, and what you can be paid for—into a personalised Ikigai statement designed to your own definition of success.

In the next few pages I have outlined simple, yet guided steps to follow that will help you through the process. However, make sure to reflect deeply and use this exercise to clarify your life's purpose and design a career that brings you fulfillment.

Step 1: Be Honest!

This is the hard part. You have to be completely honest with yourself when you walk through each of the sections. The more honest you are, the better and more accurate the outcome will be in finding your own Ikigai, aligned with your own definition of success.

Under each section, I have added some prompts for you to consider. Take your time in answering these questions. Consider this as a design process. You do not need to rush, and yes, it will take multiple revisions to perfect this.

So let's get started – and feel free to write straight on to the pages of your book. After all, this is about designing your own definition of success, so make this book your own!

What You Love: Start by identifying activities, interests, or subjects that bring you joy and excitement.

Prompts to Consider:
- *What activities make you lose track of time?*
- *What topics do you enjoy learning or talking about?*
- *When do you feel most alive or in flow?*

What the World Needs: This element focuses on how you can make a positive impact on others or address societal needs. The mission that gets you wired to go on!

Prompts to Consider:
- *What problems in the world concern you most?*
- *How can your unique abilities or passions help others?*
- *What changes do you wish to see in your community or the world?*

What You Are Good At: Next, reflect on your talents, skills, and strengths.

Prompts to Consider:
- *What skills come naturally to you, or have you developed over time?*
- *What do others often come to you for help with?*
- *What makes you feel confident and accomplished?*

What You Can Be Paid For: Now think about the areas where you can build a career or generate income. At the end of the day, you also need to make a living!

Prompts to Consider:
- *What services or products do people pay for related to your skills?*
- *In what industries are your talents valuable?*
- *What are potential business opportunities or career paths where you can earn a living?*

Step 2: The Intersections!

The hard part is done. Now it's time for pattern recognition and identify where the circles overlap. Once again, take your time to consider each of answers and focus on the following intersections in the order I have outlined:

Passion (Overlap of 'What You Love' and 'What You Are Good At') - What activities make you happy and confident?

Mission (Overlap of 'What You Love' and 'What the World Needs') - How can you align your passions with contributing to the greater good?

Profession (Overlap of 'What You Are Good At' and 'What You Can Be Paid For') - What roles or opportunities utilize your skills and offer financial reward?

Vocation (Overlap of 'What the World Needs' and 'What You Can Be Paid For') - How can you serve others in a way that provides income?

Step 3: Design Your Ikigai (The Center)

Was that a valuable experience? If you have walked through it patiently and honestly, then you might be experiencing a sense of clarity about your future, your own self, your definition of success.

Now, let's focus on the central point where all four elements intersect. This is your Ikigai! This is it! The sweet spot where it all comes together. The convergence. The core. The gooey centre. This may take time to form clearly, however, this is why we call it a design process. It will evolve as you will change, grow and experience life. Considering the prompts below, write down a simple sentence or statement that captures your Ikigai.

Prompts to consider:
- *How can you combine your passions, talents, and societal impact into a career or life path?*
- *What opportunities allow you to live in alignment with all four elements?*

Example Ikigai Sentence:

"I use my skills in [What You Are Good At] to [What the World Needs] through [What You Can Be Paid For], all while staying true to my love for [What You Love]."

My Ikigai (Revision 1)

_____

_____

_____

_____

_____

Date: _____/_____/_____

Once you've written your Ikigai statement, take a moment to reflect on it. Does it feel true to who you are and what you want to contribute to the world? If not, revisit each circle and adjust until your statement feels right. I always recommend doing this over a few weeks as an initial starting point and once you are beginning to live your Ikigai, you can revisit this yearly (this is my preference! Kind of a design checkpoint for my own life!)

A moment of gratitude...

Now that you've done the hard work. You should pat yourself on the back for taking these steps. Consider it a privilege to be able to actively find your ikigai and design your own definition of success & career, consciously.

Conscious gratitude for where you are in life is an amazing opportunity to: 1. Enjoy the present, and 2. Find the rocket fuel to your motivation in taking the next steps.

So, what should you do next? Well, it's time to Incorporate it into your definition of success and take action! Set SMART goals aligned with your Ikigai to move toward a fulfilling career and life. Whether it's learning new skills, pivoting in your career, or contributing to a cause you believe in, use this newfound clarity to guide your decisions.

Making Career Transitions

Sometimes, the discovery of an Ikigai leads people to a career (or education) transition. Moving into work that better aligns with your purpose can be a big shift, and will usually need some intense training and probably a drop in pay! But often, it's the only path to genuine fulfilment. Start by taking small steps toward change: research fields that align with your values, talk to people who are already working in those areas, and set small, achievable, and SMART milestones to build your confidence. Cultivating the courage to embrace change and adapt is a key part of the Ikigai mindset, helping you stay open to possibilities and creating a career that's not just successful on the surface but meaningful to you at its core.

Now you have all the tools required to design your own definition of success.

#inspired

END

INSPIRED SUCCESS

DESIGNING YOUR OWN DEFINITION OF SUCCESS

You eventually become the books you read, the people you listen to. So make sure it is the right books and the right voices.

Rashan Senanayake
@rashansenanayake
www.RashanSenanayake.com

THE START?

READ

DESIGNING YOUR OWN DEFINITION OF SUCCESS

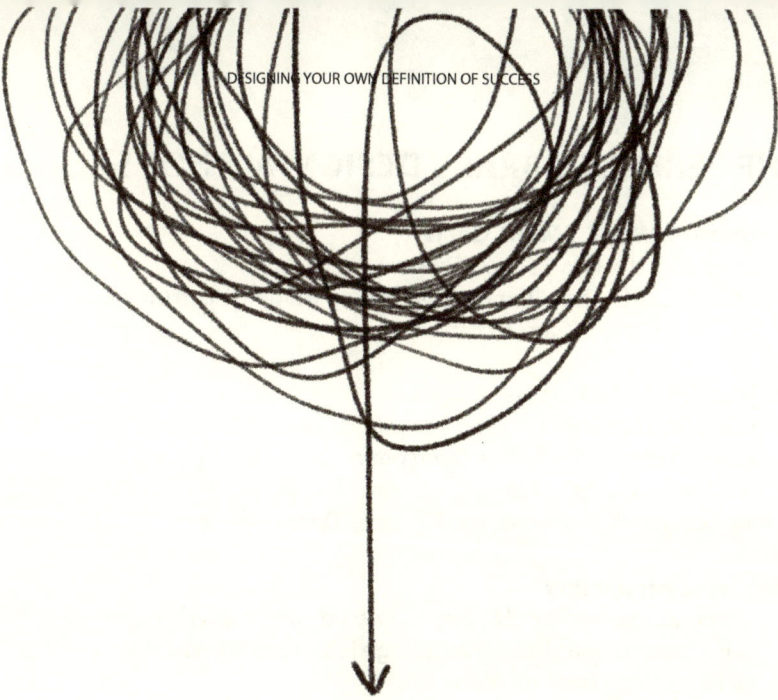

THE PERFECT LIBRARY DESIGN: AUTHOR'S READS

Chapter 1-4: Why & SMART Goals
- Start with the Why - *Simon Sinek*
- SMART Goals: The Ultimate Goal Setting Guide - *Jacob Gudger*
- Find your Why - *Peter Docker*

Chapter 5: Self Awareness
- Think and Grow Rich - *Napoleon Hill*
- Get Out of Your Own Way: Overcoming Self-Defeating Behavior - *Mark Soulston & Phillip Goldberg*
- Working with Emotional Intelligence - *Daniel Goleman*

Chapter 6: Personality
- Do What You Are - *Paul D. Tieger, Barbara Barron & Kelly Tieger*
- The Personality Brokers: The Strange History of Myers-Briggs and the Birth of Personality Testing - *Merve Emre*
- How to Win Friends and Influence People - *Dale Carnegie*

Chapter 7: Motivation
- 7 Habits of Highly Effective People - *Stephen R . Covey*
- The Power of Positive Thinking - *Norman Vincent Peale*
- Power of Now - *Eckhart Tolle*

Chapter 8: Learning Styles
- The Art of Learning - *Josh Waitzkin*
- The First 20 Hours: How to Learn Anything, Fast! - *Josh Kaufman*
- Design for How People Learn - *Julie Dirksen*

Chapter 9: Values, Morals & Ethics
- The Road to Character - *David Brooks*
- The Moral Landscape - *Sam Harris*
- Beyond Good and Evil, and On the Genealogy of Morals - *Friedrich Nietzsche*
- The Power of Ethics - *Susan Liautaud*
- How to Be Perfect - *Michael Schur*

Chapter 10: Body
- Different Bodies, Different Diets - *Carolyn Mein*
- Habits of a Happy Brain - *Loretta Graziano*

Chapter 11: Nutrition
- Nutrition in Crisis - *Richard D. Feinman*
- Good to go - *Christie Ashwanden*
- The Complete Book of Ketones - *Mary Newport*

- Eat to Love - *Jenna Hollenstein*

Chapter 12: Intermittent Fasting
- Neurofitness - *Dr. Jandial*
- Delay, Don't Deny: Living an Intermittent Fasting Lifestyle - *Gin Stephens*
- The Complete Guide to Fasting - *Dr. Jason Fun and Jimmy Moore*

Chapter 13: Movement & Exercise
- 3 Body Types - *C.K. Miller*
- Your Body Your Yoga - *Bernie Clare*
- The 4-Hour Body - *Timothy Ferriss*

Chapter 14: Mental Health
- The Gifts of Imperfection - *Brene Brown*
- UNFU*K Yourself - *Gary John Bishop*
- The Subtle Art of Not Giving a F*ck - *Mark Manson*

Chapter 15: Gratitude
- Words of Gratitude for Mind, Body, and Soul - *Robert Emmons & Joanna Hill*
- The Gratitude Diaries - *Janice Kaplan*

Chapter 16: Letting Go
- The Power of Now - *Eckhart Tolle*
- The Art of Happiness - *Dalai Lama*
- You Can Heal Your Life - *Louise L. Hay*

Chapter 17: Stress
- The Upside of Stress: Why stress is good for you and how to get good at it - *Kelly McGonigal*
- Don't Sweat the Small Stuff - *Richard Carlson*
- How to Stop Worrying and Start Living - *Dale Carnegie*

Chapter 18: Mindfulness
- 10% Happier - *Dan Harris*
- Where You Go, There You Are - *Jon Kabat-Zinn*
- The Power of Now - *Eckhart Tolle*

Chapter 19: Resilience
- Grit - *Angela Duckworth*
- Resilience - *Eric Grietens*
- Developing Resilience: A Cognitive Behavioural Approach - *Michael Neenan*

Chapter 20: Success Mindset
- Mindset: The new psychology of success - *Carol S. Dweck*
- How to Fail - *Elizabeth Day*
- The Squiggly Career - *Helen Tupper & Sarah Ellis*

Chapter 21: Time Management
- Deep work - *Cal Newport*
- The 4-hour Work Week - *Tim Ferriss*
- 168 Hours: You Have More time than you think - *Laura Vanderkam*
- The 80-20 Principle - *Richard Koch*

Chapter 22: Habits for Success
- Atomic Habits - *James Clear*
- The Power of Habit - *Charles Duhigg*
- Daily Rituals: How Artists Work - *Mason Currey*

Ikigai
- Ikigai: The Japanese Secret to a Long and Happy Life

Other Essential Reads:
- The Richest Man in Babylon - *George Samuel Clason*
- Good to Great - *James C. Collins*
- Steve Jobs - *Walter Isaacson*
- Losing My Virginity - *Richard Branson*
- Rich Dad, Poor Dad - *Robert Kiyosaki*
- The Art of Public Speaking - *Dale Carnegie*
- The 48 Laws of Power - *Robert Greene*

And of course, the one you are holding right now:

- **Inspired Success: Designing Your Own Definition of Success** - *Rashan Senanayake*

Sixty-eight perfect books, right alongside your Inspired Success journey map. A roadmap to learning from the best of the best entrepreneurs, business leaders, authors, thought leaders, experts, athletes, and other successful individuals is now right at your fingertips.

To own this entire library, it will cost you approximately $1500 to own each hard copy. However, the return of investment from these books is limitless. 10x? 100x? 1000x? 10000x? That is up to you.

THE START?

LISTEN

DESIGNING YOUR OWN DEFINITION OF SUCCESS

THE AUDIOBOOK

Exclusive to **audible**
an amazon company

Narrated by the author, the audiobook of Inspired Success: Designing Your Own Definition Of Success, extends from the print version to include a podcast style discussion, after each chapter.

Tune into Audible to extend the learnings through the audiobook.

THE PODCAST

| Listen on **Spotify** Podcasts | Listen on **Apple Podcasts** | Listen on **YouTube Music** |

Inspiring Design, the podcast is the missing link where design and education meet. Our guests sharing their knowledge in design, design education, design thinking, teaching techniques, industry standards, as well as the study of design, connecting the knowledge gaps in the design industry from a secondary, tertiary and industry standpoint.

It's the way to transform new realities, enabling new futures.

These are the top 11 most popular episodes of Inspiring Design, chosen by the author himself. All episodes can be found on *www.rashansenanayake.com/*podcast or on **Apple Podcasts, Spotify, Youtube Music and more.**

PS: You should listen in this success order!

- **Resilience - The Power of Perspective** with Michael Crossland (S03: Ep 05)
- **Foundational Principles of Success** with Michael Lane (S03: Ep 09)
- **The 5 Inner Critics and How These Design our Life** with Shade Zahrai (S03: Ep 21)
- **The Importance of Creativity and Innovation** with Adam Hudson (S03: Ep 07)
- **Skills Currency - The Foundation of 21st Century Career Success** with Leanne Kemp (S01: Ep 22)
- **Mindfulness in 21st Century Education** with Amy Lou Wilson (S03: Ep 18)
- **The Future of Work and the Key Ingredients for Success** with Lavinia Iosub (S03: Ep. 04)
- **The Importance of Failing Forward** with Shelby Parkes (S02: Ep 09)
- **Year 4 to NASA - A Pathway Beyond This World** with Megha Wijewardane (S02: Ep 05)
- **Designing Ethical Communication** with Ryan Tuckwood (S03: Ep 16)
- **Investing in the 21st Century** with Nathan Birch (S03: Ep: 22)

Tune in to Inspiring Design for more amazing episodes and learning opportunities.

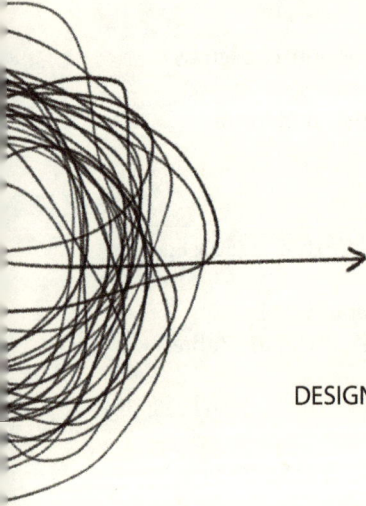

IT'S TIME TO

START

DESIGNING YOUR OWN DEFINITION OF SUCCESS

SUCCESS DESIGN CHECKLIST

Congratulations on selecting this book to help you inspire and design your own definition of a successful life. One of the most important things you can do is take action, however slowly, to keep consistently moving forward to the life of your dreams. For those of you who love checklists and ticking things off… the 'Design Checklist' below allows you to begin taking action and start… right now.

THE START!	Finish reading this book!	✓
	Start your Perfect Library Design	
	Listen to Top 11 Podcast Episodes to learn from the best!	
PART 1: **Why?**	Look for and find your 'Why'	
	Write it down and refine it every 6 months	
	Plan and turn them into (short and long term) Goals for your life	
	Set up SMART Goals to design your path	
PART 2: **Self-Awareness**	Study and understand your personality type and traits	
	Study and learn your own values	
	Clarify your ethical principles and moral compass	
	Study and uncover your learning styles	
	Practice and develop habits to set fire to your motivation traits	
PART 3: **Body**	Understand and observe your body	
	Design healthy body practices	
	Audit your pantry / fridge and eating habits	
	Set up good nutrition habits	
	Practice a nutrition plan that fits your lifestyle	
	Drink water (consistently, everyday!)	
	Set up regular movement and exercise routines	
	Set up a space to consistently use	
	Move! Exercise! (consistently!)	
PART 4: **Mind & Body**	Understand and observe your mental health	
	Understand why it's important to practice gratitude, mindlessness and develop resiliency	
	Practice gratitude	
	Practice mindfulness activities	
	Manage your stress through guided activities	
	Build your resilience and self esteem	
PART 5: **Taking Action**	Set up practices to manage your time and refine periodically	
	Understand a growth mindset and build habits towards establishing this mindset	
	Practice and develop a success mindset and success habits	
	Never Quit!	✓

INSPIRED INDIVIDUALS

"This is a powerful book dedicated to people who are seeking their own authentic success."

The success game has completely changed, success in a 2021 world is less about money and more about impact. Inspired Success covers the fundamentals of new world success and is a vital tool in determining how you see your success.

Rashan is a master at holistically breaking down how to create abundance in your life. I recommend this book for anyone wanting to change the world with their ideas.

Michael Lane
Managing Director of Success Resources Australia

"A simple & actionable guide for a fulfilling life."

"This is not your typical self-help book. In a society characterised by information-overload, Rashan has crafted an essential guidebook covering the foundational elements a young person needs to lead a fulfilling life. This simple to read and actionable guide will undoubtedly help many and have lasting impact!"

Shadé Zahrai
Director Influenceo Global, Personal Mastery Expert & Best-selling Author

---

"An evocative, powerful read - essential for any young person trying to navigate their own way successfully through life"

"An evocative, powerful read - essential for any young person trying to navigate their own way successfully through life. Rashan has a unique ability to guide his readers through a journey, to empower them to take the driving seat in their own life. Highly recommend every school leaver and 20-something person reads this!"

Anna Ball
Director of Dot & Quill, Mother and Loving Wife

"A great road map to navigate the complexity of our new reality."

"Considering that the average millennial will have over 12 jobs in their lifetime, the traditional linear career path is no longer a reality. It is therefore essential for graduates to be adaptable, resilient and grounded in their values and self-concept. "Inspired Success: Designing your own Success" is a very practical and considered book, on how one might manage themselves in preparation for the volatile economic conditions that have defined the current state of employability in Australia and across the globe. In this book, many known self-management techniques are discussed but in a way that makes them accessible to a core audience of primarily recent graduates and those in their final year of tertiary studies. In this way, the author has attempted to give the graduate facing such unprecedented uncertainty, with a practical 'road-map' covering such ground as 'self-awareness, motivation and values.' This road map can effectively assist students and grads with building key 'soft skills' that will enable them to thrive in their post-university career paths.

Lisa Scharoun
Head of School - QUT School of Design, Academic, Design Researcher & Visual Designer

---

"Inspired Success is your one-stop-read to truly defining success for yourself."

"From goal setting to mental health to creating a successful mindset, Inspired Success is your one-stop-read to truly defining success for yourself. Rashan is not only an experienced being, but an impeccable writer who has been able to lay out the steps of finding success in a simple, easy to read book that captures your mind from the first page all the way to the last. This book is highly recommended for anyone, of any age group, looking to challenge themselves and take action to create a more meaningful, fruitful life.

Shiv Rad
Author of "The Regular Effect"

"Inspired Success is a powerful book teaching resilience, how to face obstacles and change management."

"Rashan Senanayake takes us on a remarkable journey through the minds of successful individuals. Inspired Success is a powerful book teaching resilience, how to face obstacles and change management. Anyone who wants to re - engineer their minds and shift to the next level should read this book."

Megha Wijewardane
Australia's only NASA Ambassador & youngest NASA ambassador in the world

---

" Inspired Success is 'inspiring'. "

"Inspired Success is 'inspiring'. Rashan has been able to capture the framework for future success in a way that is easy to read and implement, that captivates readers of all ages as they chart their pathway in an increasingly changing and innovative world. The book is rich with experience and guidance, to enable the reader to design their own success, and work toward achieving it. This book is highly recommended for students through to people in their 20's who want to be able to navigate their own journey, to find the success that is right for them."

Russell Lidgard
Head of Department – 21st Century Learning, Father and Design Thinker

---

"A go-to guide to design a successful life - no matter what success means to you."

"Inspired Success is an informative, inspiring, and motivational read that leads any reader to take action in living all aspects of a well-designed life. Rashan was able to condense the best topics of personal development and well-being in one place, making it easy for everyone to digest the ideas and implement them. As a mum to two kids, I'm grateful for having this book available. I recommend it to all teenagers and young adults who want to live in integrity and who are experiencing a transitional phase in their lives, where choices and decisions need to be made."

Helena Miceli
Mum, Life Design Mentor, Holistic Counsellor & Meditation Therapist

"Your road map to living an inspired and goal-driven life starts right here."

"It's like having a mentor in your pocket - an essential guide on living an inspired life for every human, regardless of age, living in this fast-paced and competitive modern world. Rashan shares practical and relatable advice and easy tools to help navigate and find your why to achieve success. If you are just starting out on this journey, this is a great starting guide - to put it simply, a road map!"

Winnie Nguyen
Emerging Public Health leader, Circular Economy Activator, Curator - World Economic Forum Global Shapers Gold Coast

---

"Totally indispensable for anyone leaving high school. Rashan has architected a road map to success, just add inspiration and action."

"With Inspired Success, Rashan has done what you would expect from an A+ student... over delivered. In his masterpiece, you will find everything you need to architect an amazing life from someone I truly admire. Unsure of what you are missing in your diet? It's covered. Wondering how and why your life goals are leaving you flat footed and uninspired? Solved. But, reader beware - there is work to be done. Lucky for you, you have Rashan expertly guiding you through exercises designed to guarantee your success."

Dan Jeffs
Exercise Physiologist , Founder of MyIdealHealth

"A head-start to designing your success with Inspired Success."

"A brilliant and upbeat read, encapsulating a journey sprinkled with light-hearted anecdotes within reflective and powerfully evocative content on designing one's success, especially for young people growing up in a highly dynamic and innovative environment. Rashan has used rich personal experiences to engage and inspire his audience. Highly recommended for all yearning to succeed."

Sharon Singh
International Educator (CS & IT); Head of eLearning & Innovation, Wife, Mother & Grandmother

"An equally motivational and practical guide to defining and achieving your own success"

"They say it takes years to become an overnight success. "Inspired Success" offers you the concepts, frameworks and practical advice you need in order to design your own 'definition' of success - and the life of your dreams.
It is less like a book, and more like an in-depth personal development bootcamp with yourself (which would normally cost you many thousands of dollars). It touches upon all of life's important aspects, from nutrition, emotional intelligence, exercise, to stress management and spirituality, complete with further reading and actionables after each chapter.
Inspired Success is highly recommended for any young person who wants to be happy and successful, forge their own path in the world and make a difference."

Lavinia Iosub
Managing Partner - Livit International, Founder - Remote Skills Academy, Future of Work Enthusiast

---

"Your guide to success."

"Inspired Success" is a fantastic resource for those wishing to guide themselves from where they are, to where they want to be. Rashan has managed to capture his personality and what he brings as an educational expert in Innovative Thinking practices and put it into a resource for all to access. If you find yourself at the beginning of your journey or you are already on your way, this book is a fantastic guide to help you along the way."

Paul Doneley
Head of Technologies, Husband, Father, Coach

AUTHOR'S DISCLAIMER

The author humbly acknowledges that he is not an expert in all the discussed areas and that this book may not be applicable to everyone. It is designed for anyone who is willing to and seeking to design their own definition of success – young or old!

The learnings in this book are what has worked for the author and are constantly being refined and evolved – the same as for you, and every world-renowned mentor. However, the foundational principles are the same. The patterns for success are the same.

So, Rashan wrote a book about it – to help others similar to himself.

However, the same as designing a house, you would not simply copy another person's house design and call it your home! Therefore, it is about learning from others and creating your own 'home'. Consult expert and professional advice, self-reflect and adjust, refine to suit your own life, your own context.

#inspired

ABOUT THE AUTHOR

Rashan is inspiring innovation & emerging technologies around Australia as the founder and CEO of Australia's leading professional development for 21st century education & industry: Inspired Education Australia.

In addition to this, Rashan is also the Design Director for Inspired Design Australia, servicing and helping other entrepreneurs, start-ups and small to medium businesses with 'Design for Business'.

Rashan delivering a keynote at a National Education Conference.

Rashan, originally from Sri Lanka, migrated to Australia at a young age, where he cultivated a passion for design and demonstrated strong leadership skills throughout his secondary and tertiary education. Pursuing his love for design, Rashan embarked on a journey to become a practicing Architect, earning a Bachelor of Design (Architecture) with First-Class Honours from Queensland University of Technology (QUT) in 2011. He went on to complete his Master of Architecture in 2012, graduating among the top 10 of his cohort. However, Rashan soon transitioned from traditional architectural practice to focus on shaping the future of Australian education, using his expertise to inspire and empower the next generation.

Rashan has established a strong reputation for his entrepreneurial mindset and leadership across diverse industries and projects. As a published author of 'Inspired Success: Designing Your Own Definition Of Success' and an international speaker, he has delivered impactful content to many stakeholders, schools, universities and businesses and has been a sought-after voice at global conferences, seminars, keynotes, and lectures for many years. Rashan's insights have been featured on various podcasts, in design journals, and in academic publications across Australia. His podcast, Inspiring Design, consistently ranks among the top 200 education podcasts globally and has been Australia's leading design and technology education resource for schools since 2021.

In addition to his contributions to industry and education, Rashan is an academic at Queensland University of Technology (QUT), where he teaches Design, Design Thinking, and Architecture. He is an Associate Fellow of the Higher Education Academy and engages with global initiatives as a Global Shaper Alumni for the World Economic Forum (WEF) and a member of the United Nations Association of Australia (UNAA) Queensland Chapter. Previously, he was the youngest board member of the Australian Green Development Forum (AGDF), further showcasing his commitment to sustainability and innovation.

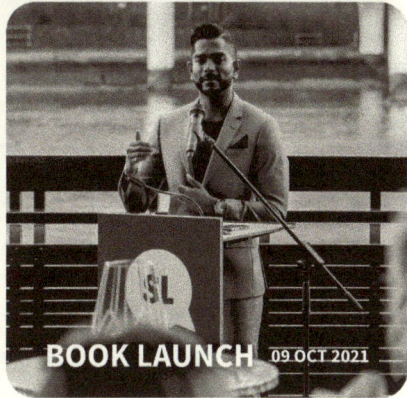

Top: 300+ high achieving students at QUT's Future You Summit holding the gifted copy of this book. **Bottom Left:** Audiobook production at the studio. **Bottom Right:** Rashan speaking at the book launch at the Queensland State Library.

Most importantly, Rashan is a firm believer in encouraging young people to see that designing their own life is not just possible, but realistic – and this book is a testament to his desire to help action this dream.